Taking Over

EDDIE LONG

CREATION
HOUSE

TAKING OVER by Eddie Long
Published by Creation House
Strang Communications Company
600 Rinehart Road
Lake Mary, Florida 32746
Web site: http://www.creationhouse.com

Unless otherwise noted, all Scripture quotations are
from the New King James Version of the Bible.
Copyright © 1979, 1980, 1982 by Thomas Nelson, Inc.,
publishers. Used by permission.

Library of Congress Cataloging-in-Publication Data
Long, Eddie L.
    Taking over / by Eddie L. Long.
        p. cm.
    ISBN: 0-88419-484-1
    1. Church renewal. I. Title.
BV600.2.L63 1999
269—dc21   98-28750
                                                    CIP

9 0 1 2 3 4 5 6 BBG 8 7 6 5 4 3 2 1
Printed in the United States of America

This book is dedicated to . . .

*My father, Rev. Floyd Long, who has gone
on to his eternal reward, and my mother,
Hattie Long, who is the reason I am
where I am today.*

ACKNOWLEDGMENTS

To my wife, Vanessa—you pay a dear price for sharing your husband with so many. I want you to know how much I appreciate you and love you for who you are and all that you do. Thank you for your love, support, understanding, and sacrifice.

To my children, Edward, Jared, and Taylor—you have sacrificed much in order that I might write this book. Sharing your father with so many is not easy, and I love each of you very much. Thank you!

To my executive assistant and friend, Everett Gates—you have been with me through all the changes and trials of ministry. Thank you for your ability to stand in the midst of confusion and to bring order out of chaos.

To Jeremy Upton—thank you for walking with me and assisting me with this project, I love you, son!

To Brother Larry Walker—thank you for surrendering your talents and gifts for the kingdom's sake.

But most of all, I thank God, for in Him I live, I move, and I have my being.

CONTENTS

FOREWORD

If God were to render judgment on His church today, sadly we would get a low grade. Oh yes, we know how to have church; some of us even know how to praise and worship God. In some places we have witnessed awesome signs, wonders, healings, and miracles because of the anointing. However, if God's agenda and order are not being promoted, then we have failed God.

In the past decade there has been a move of God that is requiring our houses of worship to come in line with the Word of God and to reflect the power and authority of God—or else lose His favor. However, the same is not the case outside the house of God, where there is little or no respect for the authority of God. It's not because God is limited or lacking in His power, but because we, the body of Christ, have taken on a deferential posture toward every institution in our society. We water down. We compromise. We placate. We've been acting like the tail instead of the head, when we've been called to be the head. But this must stop.

Our God, Jesus' Father, is not merely the God of the church; He is the God of the universe. The psalmist tells us, "The earth is the LORD's, and all its fullness" (Ps. 24:1). *Everything* falls under God's authority. This is where the whole notion of the separation of church and state fails.

No one has helped us to understand this better than Bishop Eddie Long. I admire him for his courage and boldness to speak up and speak out the truth in this area, when so many others have ducked and dodged it for fear of ridicule and alienation. Our nation and our churches continue to cry out for this type of leadership—leadership that respects the authority of God and follows the mandates of the gospel of Jesus Christ.

During his lifetime, my father, Dr. Martin Luther King, Jr., held the notable distinction of being the moral leader of America. In that role, he challenged all of us to be whom God called us to be. It has been thirty-one years since his assassination, and no other Christian leader has distinguished himself in quite the same vein. There have been "voices crying in the wilderness," but few have been heard, for "many are called, but few are chosen." I believe that Bishop Long is one of the few chosen by God to draw our attention back to God and His way of doing things.

As we approach the new millennium, Bishop Long's voice and message will propel the body of Christ to the forefront of every segment of our American society. We will listen and take heed, not merely because his message is biblically accurate and precise, but because he has successfully developed a ministry that is a force with which to be reckoned. Whenever you grow a church from a few hundred to over twenty thousand in less than ten years and survive the victimization that often accompanies this kind of phenomenal growth, you cannot be, nor should you be, ignored. I believe that more and more of us, church leaders in particular, will be referring and defer-ring to the leadership of Bishop Eddie Long and his ministry at New Birth for our marching orders. I say "marching orders" because we are at war with Satan and his imps, and we will lose if we don't know how to pre-pare and how to position ourselves for this war.

God has given His church a mandate and a mission to take over, and He has given it to us through the voice and hand of Bishop Long in this book you are holding. Now that you have picked it up, please don't let go of it. Your life is about to change. Your attitude is about to change.

In this book, Bishop Long defines what the church of the new millennium must look like from the inside out in order to be powerful and respected. With the use of per-sonal ministry experiences, he talks with candor about his journey from being a timid preacher to a now pow-erful and bold bishop over an expansive ministry. He discusses the value of transparency to growing an effec-tive ministry. He also warns us of the danger of aligning ourselves with others when it may call for compromising the gospel of Jesus Christ, thus watering down its trans-forming power. If you are a pastor or church leader, pay particular attention to chapter eight on the transgenera-tional transfer of the heart and Spirit of God. You will glean insight into how to keep alive the vision God has given you, even after you are gone.

My prayer is that once you have read the last word, you will never be the same. Your witness will become more radical; you will begin to take your rightful place as a son or daughter of God. Before this book, you may not have understood your purpose in the earth, and that's why you've been timid and tentative. After this book, you will not only know better, but you will do better. The precepts and principles discussed will ignite your spirit and cause you to walk in the authority that God has granted you—the authority "to have dominion over." Not only in this generation, but for generations to come.

Open your heart and mind as Bishop Long takes you from the posture of being overtaken to *taking over*. You and I are about to reveal God's kingdom all over this land. The true church is about to *take over*. Thank you, Bishop Long, for getting our attention and for stirring us up.

—BERNICE A. KING
ASSISTANT TO PASTOR
GREATER RISING STAR BAPTIST CHURCH
ATLANTA, GEORGIA

I am here to take over, not to take sides.
I have come to take over, and I have
   no room for compromise.
This is a whole new way of life; this is
   a whole new way of thinking.
This is a whole new way of opera-
   tion, and when you get that settled,
You're presenting kingdom.

1

TAKING OVER

W hat man would say something like the words on the previous page? I can think of a few. One was fathered by a priest, lived in a desert, ate insects and honey, and wore animal skins. He called some of the leading preachers of his day "snakes" and told everyone to repent and be baptized in a muddy river if they wanted to be clean.

Another was conceived by an unwed mother, born in a barn, and raised by a carpenter who wasn't His real father. This man dared to say that God was His Father and that He was on a mission from God. He knew that comment would get Him killed—but it didn't stop Him.

Many more have followed in the confrontational footsteps of John the Baptist and Jesus, including me. Something changed and transformed me when I heard my Father in heaven say to my spirit, "My charge never changed." God reminded me that in the very beginning, in the Book of Genesis, He gave man a mandate:

> Then God blessed them, and God said to them, "Be fruitful and multiply; fill the earth and subdue it; have dominion over the fish of the sea, over the birds of the air, and over every living thing that moves on the earth."
>
> —GENESIS 1:28

Early in my Christian life I was very insecure, but something moved me from timidity to boldness! What possessed me to launch the opening session of the Georgia State Senate with an altar call? How could I dare to stand before the full U.S. Senate in Washington, D.C., and tell our senators that the U.S. government in its current state is an "illegitimate government" because it has rejected the authority of God's Word?

What right do I have to say, "I'm here to take over, not take sides"?

It doesn't come from my credentials, my training, or my personal accomplishments. My authority to say such things doesn't come from anything I have done or from any particular gift or ability that I possess. It comes from the Word of God and the destiny God sovereignly ordained for us. I am one of God's many "scarred" leaders who were chosen for their brokenness and weaknesses instead of their strengths. My authority comes from God's inexplicable decision to send me to the church and the nation with a message.

I don't have a big head; I have an omnipotent Father who is ready to repossess what is His and judge what isn't. I didn't write this book to impress you or anyone else; I wrote it at God's command because He wanted you and countless others to hear the same things He has been speaking to me about taking over instead of being overtaken.

My claims about "taking over" aren't ego driven,

although many might say so. They are totally Bible based, and they are said in a spirit of brokenness. The truth is that God's greatest anointing for ministry to others seems to flow at its strongest when we share our past hurts, failures, and mistakes—not when we focus on our accomplishments. Even God Himself felt it was important that He personally identify with the pains and sorrows of mankind before He could set us free, so who are we to second-guess God?

REVISITING THE LOWEST POINTS IN MY LIFE

The Lord has called us to challenge some of the most powerful institutions and traditions in the church and in the American political scene, and we have begun the fight. Yet He often takes us, myself included, back to some of the lowest points in our lives to keep our feet firmly planted on the Rock.

The beginning of my ministry in my twenties was a tangle of pain, missteps, and a deep longing for God's purposes. My major failures started with my first sermon, and they include a divorce and the loss of a six-figure income after being fired by one of America's top ten corporations. My successes all seem to stem from the lessons I learned in those early years of struggle and searching.

I grew up in the Baptist tradition, and I managed to overcome my early timidity enough to become a successful factory sales representative for Ford Motor Company. The people who recruited me for the job made it clear that I was expected to "cheat" on expense reports because "everybody did it." But I somehow made an enemy or came into disfavor, and those same reports were used to justify my firing because I included some personal long distance phone calls on one. (My parishioners seem to relate to me better knowing their pastor has committed the sin of lying and has paid a price for it.)

TAKING OVER

"GOD, IF YOU DO THIS, THEN I'LL DO THAT"

I moved on to the Honeywell Corporation and again rose quickly to the top ranks of the corporate sales force, all the while wrestling with God's call to the ministry. I felt the call, but I either made excuses or tried to "set things up" by negotiating with the Lord: "Well, God, if You do this, then I'll do that." The final frontier was defined by my manipulative prayer, "Lord, if You send me a wife, I'll do it. I'll go into the ministry, but I've got to have somebody like my mom."

A couple of days later I met a girl, and I swore up and down that she was from God. To make a very long story very short, on the day I delivered my first "trial sermon," I also introduced this woman to the congregation and said, "God sent me this young lady." After the wedding, we hadn't even left the church building before this woman turned to me and basically said, "I just wanted to see if I could get you."

Our marriage lasted for three years, during which time a son was born to us; those three years were difficult times at best. Although I still wanted to make our marriage work, my wife filed for divorce anyway, leaving me broken spiritually, emotionally, and in every other way you can think of.

I can recall vividly the day I just stopped my car in the middle of the road and asked God, "Why?" He spoke to my spirit and said, "Son, do not ever tell Me what you need when I tell you to do something. From this point on, whenever I speak to you, *you do it,* and I will supply what you need along the way." I have never forgotten that.

God was true to His Word, even in the middle of problems I had created by my own presumption. I was a newly divorced part-time Baptist preacher entangled in a devastating child custody battle, and I had lost everything due to the legal expenses. I had adopted a homeless boy named Eric before everything blew up, and he was living with me. By that time the sum of my worldly possessions consisted of a mattress, a television set, and a stereo. I had begged God in prayer, "Don't let me lose the house, Lord," but He let me lose it anyway. (I was discovering more about God's maturation process every day.) I had a day or two to get out, so I said to Eric, "Well, let's just go get a haircut."

GOD CAN EVEN FIND YOU AT THE BARBER SHOP

Eric and I were sitting in the barber shop when the barber asked me how I was doing. I said, "Well, I'll be homeless by Monday." A lady who "just happened" to overhear us told me, "You know, there is a house available across the street from me. Let me give you the address of the owner. Now look him up." Then she left.

I made the connection and was shocked to discover that the house was better than the house I was giving up. It was located in such an exclusive neighborhood that you couldn't even get in without clearance. I told the owner that I didn't have any money at the moment, but he said, "The people who used to live here left a bunch of trash in the house. If you clean it up, I'll let you have the first month free. After that you can give me four hundred dollars or something." It was *half* of what I was paying before. We moved in, and within six months we had fully furnished the house. I still can't figure out how we did that.

My point is that when God speaks to you about something, *if you do it,* then He will supply what you need along the way—even if He has to lead a stranger into your favorite barber shop or hair salon.

But this book isn't about me; it is about the purpose of God in this generation and how *you* fit into it. As you read on, I want you to say *Yes!* to God and *No!* to the limitations in your life (most of which are man-made). If you do, I can guarantee you that your life will *change,* and so will the lives of countless others around you. God's purposes are not difficult to discover. He has committed them to writing, and He continues to restate and reinforce them by His Spirit to those with ears to hear. *His charge has never changed;* it is man's agenda that has changed with every wind of adversity and hope of personal gain.

GOD MADE IT ALL, AND HE CLAIMS IT ALL

God has called the people of His kingdom to be fruitful, to multiply, to replenish the earth, and to subdue and have dominion over it. After God gave Adam that charge, he and Eve fell into sin, and Satan assumed a measure of dominion and authority over the earth as the "prince of the power of the air" (Eph. 2:2). That didn't alter or annul God's charge; it simply expanded it. Now we must subdue and have dominion over the prince of the power of the air as well as over the earth. Jesus took away Satan's keys and power at Calvary, and it is up to us to come along behind and subdue and have dominion over every evil work and every servant of evil. This can never be accomplished by a timid church that obediently hides behind the artificial walls of the so-called "separation of church and state." God doesn't recognize any such separation. He made it all, and He claims it all.

We preach a gospel of repentance and love, but we should declare that gospel with boldness. Jesus refused to hide Himself behind the walls of the temple or inside a comfortable house in Bethsaida. He boldly marched into crowded city squares and into the temple of Herod to physically toss out the moneychangers and animal vendors. He publicly rebuked and embarrassed powerful religious and political leaders because His Father told Him to do so. Jesus didn't come to take sides or compromise; He came to destroy the works of the enemy without mercy.

He came to *take over.* Peter dared to openly defy the chief priest by declaring the truth of the gospel, and so did Stephen, James, and Paul. Every one of them died for the sake of the gospel because *they knew the gospel was something to die for!*

WE CAUSE MORE PEOPLE TO STUMBLE THAN TO STAND

I think we have made the gospel so unrealistic that it has caused more people to stumble and fall than to stand. When I say unrealistic, I am referring to our modern gospel of hypocrisy. The world outside our church walls views Christians as holier-than-thou hypocrites who preach a plastic gospel of "do's and don'ts." The world views us this way because the gospel we preach appears to have nothing to do with the difficult realities of life mixed with human weaknesses. We could use a good dose of honesty in our dealings with non-Christians.

I believe the gospel of the Bible must be preached without compromise, but our greatest ministry comes out of brokenness and transparency about our failures and pain. I am convinced that God does not even release us to minister to others until we have been broken and have come through the process with a good attitude (although we usually rush ahead of His timing).

We need to stay the course with God until we are able to stand strong in our brokenness and say, "Let me share with you about the time I made the same mistake in my life and about how God corrected it." I think the major draw of the ministry God has given me at New Birth Missionary Baptist Church is its *transparency.* One Sunday I stood up and admitted to my congregation that I was struggling with some issues. That week I received letters from people in the congregation that all said in effect, "I felt your anointing and your pain for the first time last Sunday. I know how to pray for you now."

Pastors don't generally do that, and it is to their own detriment.

YOU ARE TOO STRONG

Many times pastors who have fallen into adultery or moral problems will go to other church leaders and confess their sins. They will declare that they have been broken by their experience, and then in the same breath will say, "I want to be restored." Wise church leaders will generally tell them, "You are too strong. The same inner strength that led you to the sin will lead you there again until the day it is totally broken." Very often the "repentant" brothers will fume and complain, saying, "And I came all this way to hear that?" They are still too strong to be truly broken.

I can tell you that the only reason I am still standing in a position of leadership today is that I am willing to admit I am weak. And I have been diligent to train my spiritual sons and leaders to recognize their weaknesses and constantly acknowledge what God has done in their lives. It is my responsibility to be the most transparent leader in the church because I expect it of the leaders under me. Being in touch with the "real" you makes you a better minister.

I am the same man who experienced a broken marriage and a broken heart a number of years ago. I am the man who was only two days away from being homeless. Yet I stayed on course by God's grace, and now I lead Atlanta's largest church congregation, a flock of twenty-two thousand. Most of my people already know me, but when people first come to New Birth Missionary Baptist Church, they may be tempted to misjudge me when they look at the car I drive and the honor the people give me as their pastor and bishop. But once they find out that the same Bishop Long who now drives a Mercedes used to walk everywhere, that he knows what it is like to lose everything and come to the brink of homelessness, they think, *Oh, he's like us. He knows what it's like.*

HE KNOWS WHAT IT'S LIKE TO GIVE IN TO SIN

When people hear me admit that I was once fired by Ford Motor Company for making personal phone calls, they think, *This man wears the robes of a bishop, but he knows what it's like out in the corporate world. He knows about the pressures I face. In fact, he knows what it is like to give in to that pressure, too.* If I never shared my failures and weaknesses with people, they wouldn't think I had any credibility to talk to them about such things. I understand that when people see a preacher step behind a pulpit, they think, *What does he know?* So I tell them what I know. I tell them how God saved me. I tell them that I am a walking miracle of God who is still in awe that God could and would choose to use me. Then I start on *them*.

"Do you believe God's Word is true?"

"Yes sir, every word."

"Do you believe God loves you and has a *plan* for your life, too?"

"Yes, Bishop. I believe all of that."

"All right. Then you are *taking over,* right? If not, *why not?* Is your life being overtaken by sin? Are you choosing to do everything *but* the things God told you to do? *Why?*"

Most people in the church have a ready excuse: "You don't understand, Bishop. I've got problems."

No, *we* don't understand God's purpose for the church. We have a bigger problem than our problems! We've got a head commitment to Jesus Christ, but our hearts and bodies haven't caught up yet. It's time to get ourselves in order so we can take our place in God's plan and start living. God has given us everything we need to succeed and live a life for Jesus. No excuse will do when we stand before Him.

GOD IS LOOKING FOR SOLDIERS

The church of the living God is ordained and anointed to go into enemy territory, snatch people out of darkness, and bring them into the marvelous light. That is the primary reason why God blesses us so much. He doesn't want us to have any worries; He wants us to know that our needs are already met in Him. That is why He said in essence, "I already know what you have need of. Don't waste time praying for that." (See Matthew 6:8.) He is telling each one of us in the church:

> Get on the battlefield! Go and bring in the people who are lost. That is the reason why I delivered you from the things that bound you. You are an expert in those things now, so go out there and find those entangled in the same problems. You now have the anointing to show them how to get out. Go back into the enemy's territory, snatch them out of darkness, and bring them into the light!

God is looking for soldiers. Everybody wants to be a saint, and that's fine, but we have too many saints and not enough soldiers. We need to understand that we are in a war. No one in his right mind chooses to be in a war, but the moment you were saved you were placed on the front lines of this war. Now you have to decide whether or not you are going to fight. So many of us sing "I'm so weary, worn, and sad" every day that we get up because we don't want to fight. We wear ourselves out avoiding the very purpose for our existence. Nothing is more tiring and self-defeating than that.

I am out to do more than explain why I say what I say and do what I do. The Lord has given every church leader a mandate to call the church to a higher standard in every realm of life. I am under a burden of God to encourage you, instruct you, push you, and if necessary, offend you to move you forward to take a public stand in the name of Jesus and boldly declare to your world:

> *I am here to take over, not to take sides.*
> *I have come to take over, and I have no*
>   *room for compromise.*
> *This is a whole new way of life; this is a*
>   *whole new way of thinking.*
> *This is a whole new way of operation,*
>   *and when you get that settled,*
> *You're presenting kingdom.*

Now is the time. Yesterday is gone, and tomorrow will be too late. God is coming down to see what His creation is up to, and He intends to *take over.* You and I must take our places *now* or move aside.

2

GOD IS COMING DOWN TO SEE THE CITY

T he American church is best known for her ambitious members who want to make a name for themselves. Many of us devote all of our energies to building our own kingdoms and religious monuments, often at the expense of others in the body of Christ. In true American fashion, many of our church leaders and televangelists often excel at self-promotion, hype, and pomp and circumstance, but they fail miserably in the weightier matters of obedience to God, sacrifice, humility, service to others, and submission to God-ordained authority. That is about to change.

> And they said, "Come, let us build ourselves a city, and a tower whose top is in the heavens; let us make a name for ourselves, lest we be scattered abroad over the face of the whole earth." But the LORD came down to see the city and the tower which the sons of men had built.
> —GENESIS 11:4–5

It is time for a showdown, and it is God's turn to make His statement. If I could, I would paint a picture for you by reminding you of the time God sent fire from heaven to consume Elijah's sacrifice and altar on Mount Carmel in front of four hundred priests of Baal while all of Israel watched. We need to take off our religious spectacles and stop thinking of this historical event in 1 Kings 18 as just a Bible story. It is a chilling prophetic picture of where the church and the nation are this very moment.

Israel was the "established church" of Elijah's day. It was a nation of people who had been set apart unto God many generations earlier. They still had all the traditions of their fathers in their memory, along with all the stories of God's provision recorded in the Law and the Pentateuch (the first five books of the Old Testament). But the people of God were chasing after other gods and other pursuits. Yet the day came when they were all summoned together to make a choice, and God made a clear division between what was His and what wasn't. (It is interesting to note that God isn't against highly visible and dynamic leaders—He just insists that they be elevated by His hand, not by the hand of man, and that those leaders dynamically direct His people toward His purposes and not their own.)

THE SIN MOUNTS HIGHER WHILE THE NATION SINKS LOWER

The fire is coming again, first to God's set-apart people, because judgment begins with the house of God (1 Pet. 4:17). Then it will come to the nation. Our society has defiantly turned away from its godly roots and has busied itself building monuments and laws to honor man's ingenuity over God's. While the sin mounts higher and higher, we as a nation sink deeper and deeper into a moral and financial bankruptcy of our own making. Meanwhile, God is getting ready to "come down to the city" to see what the children of men are doing. He is about to divide the church and the nation, to make a clear separation between what is His and what isn't. I don't think we have any idea what is coming.

All of us have challenges and problems in our lives, and we know that God has already provided what we need in those areas. But I'm writing this chapter with one specific purpose—*I really want to shock you* with God's Word so you can be totally focused on the "things above" in this crucial hour.

Historians and political scientists have noticed that whenever nations, political systems, or powerful leaders run into an especially difficult internal problem, such as a failing economy, a serious division in the nation, or a dangerous loss of public support, *they start a war.* Why? Because it tends to make everyone turn away from the problem and unite together to focus on one thing.

God isn't like us, and He doesn't need to start a war. But there *is* a war going on, and we need to take the focus off ourselves and put it back on God where it belongs. You and I need to realize He has placed us on the front lines of this battle whether we like it or not.

Part of our problem is that we tend to stay in only one lane of God's Word—the "bless me" lane. We forget what Paul said about the complete purpose of God's Word: "All Scripture is given by inspiration of God, and is profitable for *doctrine,* for *reproof,* for *correction,* for *instruction* in righteousness" (2 Tim. 3:16, italics added). Now I don't remember seeing the crowds line up at the door an hour ahead of time to hear a preacher talk about any one of these four areas. I think I know why.

WE FORGET WE ARE CALLED FOR HIS PURPOSE

Most of us keep our focus fixed on our personal situations in church meetings and Bible studies, but if we don't understand the greater corporate purpose of God, then our personal situations will be very painful. Why? Because we won't be able to see how our lives fit into the larger picture of what God is orchestrating. The Bible gives us a hint about how we fit into God's larger scope of attention:

> And we know that all things work together for good
> to those who love God, to those who are the called
> according to His purpose.
> —ROMANS 8:28

The eleventh chapter of the Book of Genesis describes a people who wanted to make a name for themselves. They decided to do so by building a tower up into the heavens (we call it the Tower of Babel). They all spoke one language in those days immediately following the great flood, and they came into agreement to build a tower. What those people were really trying to do was show God that they didn't need or want Him. They could reach the heavens on their own without His help or permission.

The Hebrew word *migdal* is translated "tower" in this passage, but its fuller meaning reveals the real motives of the people. According to *Strong's Exhaustive Concordance, migdal* can mean a rostrum, a castle, or a pulpit; it comes from a root word that means "to make large (as in body, mind, estate or honor, also in pride), to advance, boast, bring up, exceed, excellent, and to increase, lift up, magnify, pass, promote." It is derived from definitions and root meanings for *tower.*

NIMROD WAS THE PRINCE OF "ATTITUDE"

As with any great endeavor, a leader was required to build this tower.

> Cush begot Nimrod; he began to be a mighty one on

the earth. He was a mighty hunter before the LORD.
—GENESIS 10:8–9

Nimrod, the son of Cush, not only led the people in the building project, but he also led them in developing a bad attitude: "Somehow, we will not allow anything like a flood to come and devastate us again. Now if we agree to build a tower and rally around it as we ascend into the heavens…" Not only did they take on the mentality that Adam and Eve had (desiring to know good and evil), they also were moving in the same exact sin (wanting to be like God, but without His help or permission). They were not just trying to be like God—they wanted to be God!

We are trying to build a Tower of Babel in our day, too. We are trying to be like God—or to be *better* than He is. If you haven't noticed, America is coming into agreement with all types of folk. We are trying to use the science and technology God gave us to do things that only God can do, including the act of creating life (though we've only been able to clone something from what already exists). We want to extend life through medicine to make up for our unwillingness to live and eat with wisdom. We don't want to live disciplined lives that include regular exercise and healthy diets, and we refuse to take care of the temple of the Holy Ghost. We want to cling to our smoking habits; we gamble that if we get lung cancer, we can get a transplant.

We are trying desperately to extend our lifespans today, and you might ask, "What is wrong with that?" On the surface there is nothing wrong with it. But the real theology and personal motivation behind this push in medicine is that we are trying to eliminate God and His laws. He gave us the original "long-life plan" centuries ago, and it consists of a godly life, wise eating habits, moderation in all things, respect for parents and those in authority, and the determination to love the Lord our God with all of our being.

But we would rather develop pills to keep us from having to exercise. We choose to eat everything we want to eat in massive quantities, then we take our high-tech, fat-burner pills and additives. We want the right to be angry at other people, eat all the high-fat foods we want, live hard day and night into our fifties or sixties, and then put all of our trust in our cardiologist to keep us alive somehow another two decades. You can laugh all you want, but it is true. We are trying to usurp the system and processes of God.

WE'RE TRYING TO LIVE UP TO OUR OWN PROPAGANDA

An honest survey of our society reveals that we are trying to become God. We're trying to live up to our own propaganda (borrowed from the Greeks) about man being the "sum of all things." We are trying to rule our own destiny; even born-again Christians have adopted the secular viewpoint that the church is supposed to join hands with any outside group claiming to have even the slightest of good intentions. Tremendous pressure has been exerted on us to link up with everyone from the NAACP (National Association for the Advancement of Colored People) to the Hundred Black Men and the Hundred White Men; from fund-raisers for Greek collegiate sororities and fraternities to virtually every civic organization in our communities, including the Kiwanis Club, the Key Club, the Rotary Club, and so on.

Without question, many of these organizations are doing commendable work of great value in our communities. I'm thankful that they exist, but honestly, the only reason they exist is because the church has failed to fulfill her destiny in the earth. Many times we think we must join together and work hand in hand to make our communities a better place, but I have to tell you that according to God's Word, that popular belief is not true! Why not let me explain.

When we say that the church must work hand in hand with these organizations for good, we automatically make God and His eternal kingdom equal to all of these man-made, secular organizations. We must understand that according to the Scriptures, we are the *head* as redeemed ambassadors of Christ. As the corporate body of Christ in the earth, we are literally the only "living thing" on this earth meant and equipped to straighten out *every problem* and *every concern* of mankind. But we must do it God's way.

God's way is centered on absolute obedience and trust in Christ, the cross, and the life-changing power of the Holy Spirit. How many wonderful civic organizations can you name that would welcome those world-changing forces and beliefs into their meetings and activities? When we understand that, it becomes obvious that we can't work within the systems of the world. God has ordained a divine order for life, governments, and the church—and this order is invisible to the natural eye. Only those who are saved and baptized into this invisible kingdom can see the order and the arrangement of God.

The church has become so mixed up and pulled in different directions by the whims of men that we have gradually adopted secular views of God and depreciated Him to "next to nothing." In other words, He and His body are now viewed by Christians and non-Christians alike as just another organization. That should explain why it is very difficult for us to make a sacrifice of time, money, or personal commitment to God—we are already giving most of our time and resources to other "worthy organizations" outside the church. We justify it by saying, "Oh, they are making society better." In actuality, society has become *worse* because we have usurped the process of God. The most any man-centered organization can do apart from Christ is to apply a pretty bandage to a terminal carcinoma.

TAKING OVER

GOD DOESN'T NEED A PARTNER

I appreciate many of these civic service organizations and the individuals who volunteer their time and resources to help others. They represent the best man has to offer outside of God and His order. But I am compelled by the Word of God to say that these individuals need to come into the house of God and lay down all their titles and agendas to take on the name "child of God." If we then joined together under the banner of Christ, all the nations of this earth would be blessed because we would tackle our tasks of service in both the power of God and the submitted and unified strength of man, the power of agreement demonstrated at the Tower of Babel. That is God's intent. That is the process of God.

Now if we become angry and agitated by that process, then so be it. Perhaps that shows how far out in the world you are. The only way to change the ills and hurts of the world genuinely and permanently is to change the hearts of people and transform their thinking through the renewing power of God's Word.

BUILDING A TOWER OF POWER OUTSIDE GOD'S KINGDOM

The community of man, the "global village of the flesh," is coming into agreement. We are essentially rallying around our common desire to build a tower of power outside God's kingdom and God's process. If we put representatives of every known civic, political, and activist group in one building, they would all fight and argue with one another until a Christian dared to stand up and say, "Christ is the answer." In a split second we would see every one of those people who were at one another's throats an instant before suddenly unite with one voice to shout down and belittle their "common enemy." The church finds unity in her faith in Jesus Christ. The world finds unity in its hatred and fear of Jesus Christ.

If we examine the way we have built up and elevated the power of our centers of culture and government, we will see that our society has established a clear pattern of usurping the authority of God in every sphere of life. The Book of Genesis places the time of Noah *before* the days of Abram. It also explains why we have so many different nations and languages today.

> And the LORD said, "Indeed the people are one and they all have one language, and this is what they begin to do; now nothing that they propose to do will be withheld from them.
>
> "Come, let Us go down and there confuse their language, that they may not understand one another's speech." So the LORD scattered them abroad from there over the face of all the earth, and they ceased building the city.
>
> Therefore its name is called Babel, because there the LORD confused the language of all the earth; and from there the LORD scattered them abroad over the face of all the earth.
>
> —GENESIS 11:6–9

Why did God come down to Babel to confuse the language of the descendants of Noah and scatter them across the earth? Because of human disobedience. God had already judged the human race with the flood of judgment in Noah's day, yet He had to split the still-rebellious human race into many nations and language groups several generations later. He would soon abandon His dealings with the many nations and instead single out a descendant of Noah's son Shem to raise up *one nation* to save the rest:

Now the LORD had said to Abram:

"Get out of your country,
From your family
And from your father's house,
To a land that I will show you.
I will make you a great nation;
I will bless you
And make your name great;
And you shall be a blessing.
I will bless those who bless you,
And I will curse him who curses you;
And in you all the families of the earth shall be
  blessed."

—Genesis 12:1–3

WE HAVE FORGOTTEN THAT GOD SAID, "I WILL..."

Look closely at this passage again and remember that this is an eternal promise. God did not say Abram was to join with all the civic organizations of the world to make all the nations blessed. God said in essence, "I am going to do a whole lot of things through you, My people, the nation of Israel, whom I have chosen. In you all the other nations that I have scattered shall be blessed. That is My plan. This is My process. Now you don't have to do anything other than be obedient to Me, because I am going to do everything else." Somehow the church has forgotten that God said, "I will..."

God has already done everything that needs to be done on this earth and in this country. All He has called us to do is be obedient. We think God needs help because *we are not being obedient,* and as a consequence, we are not seeing His provision. We run out to join up with everybody else outside God's house to fix things when God never told us, "Join up with everybody else."

I am not saying these organizations and the people in them are evil or bad. The problem is that when we join up with everybody *outside* God's order and absolute rule, *we start to compromise.* In fact, not only do we compromise, but we also dilute what God has said. It is unavoidable. The only way a kingdom based upon *absolute truth* and the *absolute rule of God* can come into agreement with anything less is to water things down. Follow me as we review the progression of man's error and God's sovereignty.

1. After the flood of judgment, the descendants of Noah once again rebelled. They tried to build a tower of exaltation, a foundation of the flesh, a ladder to the heavens, and a pulpit to preach the doctrine of the power of man, a doctrine that excluded God's influence from their lives.

2. God struck down their tower of power, broke their unity of language, and divided mankind into many nations.

3. Then God chose to raise up one nation from Abram to save the world of man.

I want us all to see this, because the well-being of the body of Christ is dependent on our hearing this message from God. We are in an age when people are once again trying to become God and are openly rebelling against His divine authority at every turn.

Everybody has an opinion, but nobody has a standard. Everybody has an opinion today. Listen to the evening news on television and radio. Watch the talk shows during the day (if you dare). The reason we have so many outrageous talk shows today is because *everybody has an opinion, but nobody has a standard.* The clear contrast between the order of God and the order of the world is revealed in Genesis 10 (Noah) and 11 (the Tower of Babel). This contrast is becoming clear in our day, too.

TAKING OVER

A DEADLY SEASON OF DECEPTION

We are living in a deadly season of deception, and the church has created an environment of gullibility to deception by failing to teach the Word of God without compromise. Christians are quicker to rally around the problems of society than the answer of Christ. We gravitate toward those who claim to have answers today because we can touch them, we can see their faces, and we can admire their human abilities. All the while God remains invisible and distant to us because we do not know Him.

Various members and factions within the church have argued with one another, and many Christian leaders have had problems with me because I oppose joining arms with outside organizations for popular pro-Black causes such as the so-called Million Man March and the Day of Atonement activities sponsored by Rev. Louis Farrakhan and the Nation of Islam. My critics cry, "We are tired of the killing. We are tired of the drugs and the corruption." I am tired of all of that too, but I'm not tired of Jesus. He has never failed us; we have failed Him. He is the answer to all of our problems, but the solutions will only come when we do things His way.

Leaders like Louis Farrakhan can rise up with a message of hope mixed with liberal doses of racial hatred, division, and devotion to Islam, and they still win substantial support from Christians. Why? Because Christians have failed to obey God's call to follow Christ's example of self-sacrifice. Many of us don't want to take the painful steps necessary to leave our comfortable suburban houses to do what God has ordained in order to supernaturally meet needs in the mean streets of the inner city. We prefer our quiet neighborhoods and our exciting church meetings ten miles away from our true place of divine service. We even have trouble stepping across the property line to share the message of Jesus with the neighbor we see every day!

WE THINK A MAN IN THE FLESH
HIRED US (HE DIDN'T)

We have compromised on our jobs and with our personal priorities. We carefully avoid any mention of the Christ who redeemed and transformed us because we are afraid we will get fired. Why? Because we think a man in the flesh hired us, totally forgetting that God's Word says it is God who gives us the power to get wealth (Deut. 8:18). God gives us our jobs and vocations so that we can be witnesses, not so that He can meet our needs. He has already taken care of our needs according to Matthew 6:24–33.

We live our lives in just as much pain and anguish as the non-Christians around us because we have forgotten our Source. We are ripe for deception by anybody who dares to stand up in front of the media claiming some kind of authority or power to make our lives easier. The problem is that we know more about our problems than we do about God's Word. As a result, we fall for the temptation to follow Satan's latest pied piper into oblivion.

I want us to understand what *God* is saying today.

Nimrod foreshadows the last great world ruler who will rise up just before God descends to the earth to usher in a millennial reign. Nimrod appeared on the scene just before God called Abram out from among the Gentiles to bring him into the Promised Land. A flood of judgment had already destroyed the world once, but Noah was saved and his descendants multiplied. Then mankind revolted against God *under the leadership of someone empowered by Satan* just before God was to perform the promise. Nimrod the false messiah inspired such an ungodly move of unity that God *Himself* came down to deal with it. We are at that point *again*.

Something or somebody is about to be elevated in the earth, and we are not going to be able to handle it by ourselves. Therefore God will once again come down to handle it Himself just before He fulfills His promise. And when He comes, He will come with fire. I am not an alarmist or a pessimist; I am a Bible-believing realist.

POLITICALLY CORRECT OR NOT, GOD IS COMING TO TAKE OVER

We don't like to think about this kind of thing. We prefer to focus on our personal problems or how to get the blessings of God. "I just need a better job, or that house or car I've always wanted. Lord, all I need is four or five credit cards and a nice wardrobe so no one will know I'm living beyond my means 'by faith.'" We don't understand what is going on. We don't even have a clue that God's purposes for the earth are completed in the Man Christ Jesus. And He will yet reign over all the earth as King of kings and Lords of lords! Whether it is politically correct or not, it is truth. God is coming to take over, not take sides.

Satan's sin has eternally limited him to the role of the great imitator, the consummate counterfeit. He *knows* that one God-Man is to reign over the earth, so he is working tirelessly to impose upon our gullible world his own "god-man" as the destined world leader. The apostle Paul warns us that:

> The coming of the lawless one is according to the working of Satan, with all power, signs, and lying wonders, and with all unrighteous deception among those who perish, because they did not receive the love of the truth, that they might be saved. And for this reason God will send them strong delusion, that they should believe the lie, that they all may be condemned who did not believe the truth but had pleasure in unrighteousness.
> —2 THESSALONIANS 2:9–12

Satan's counterfeit will assume the right to enforce all

of his dictates upon the people. Satan is setting the stage to elevate his chosen leader in the public eye with lying signs and wonders. That is why I am tired of emotional saints who follow after emotional experiences. We must follow after Christ, whether or not that includes an emotional experience on any given day.

Our nation is overwhelmed with self-made turmoil and trouble, and the people are looking for somebody to fill the void—as long as it is not Jesus Christ. A vacuum is being created, ready for a great leader to fill. We are really looking for a king. Americans want somebody—anybody—who can get behind a microphone and say, "I'm going to fix it." (That is why our presidential elections are decided totally on appearance and hype, not facts or genuine convictions.) We are looking for a man because we don't understand the principles and warnings of Genesis 12. We don't understand the promise, and even worse, we don't understand or acknowledge the Promiser.

WE ARE BUILDING THE TOWER OF BABEL AGAIN

God gives us a sneak preview of the end of the story with a picture of the End-Time "Nimrod" in the Book of Revelation:

> He causes all, both small and great, rich and poor, free and slave, to receive a mark on their right hand or on their foreheads, and that no one may buy or sell except one who has the mark or the name of the beast, or the number of his name.
>
> —REVELATION 13:16–17

Nearly every checkout counter in America now uses scanners to track our purchases and to scan our credit cards. The next step in convenience and efficiency will be to do away with cards altogether. Soon we won't have to carry currency or credit cards; we will just have to give them our hands so they can scan a number implanted or imprinted there. The world will adopt this system globally, saying, "If we never carry money, we can't be robbed; crime figures will drop." (That is one reason that national governments constantly push crime figures in front of us.)

Think about this one: The Internet and World Wide Web are being hailed as the great unifying force that will pull the world together for the common good. It will also cause us all to come under one rule eventually. Even though we cannot speak the same language face to face, we can definitely speak one language this very moment by computer. In other words, we are building the Tower of Babel again. All we need is a modern-day Nimrod to stand up and say, "See, we don't need God. We are a monument and force unto ourselves."

God is about to come down and visit this generation. He is ready to strike down our resurrected Tower of Babel once again, but this time He expects to find a remnant church, an occupation force that is obedient, faithful, and full of glory and power in the midst of the world's darkness. I am convinced that a "new and improved" version of Nimrod is about to rise up and draw an awed world together under his dazzling show of charisma and power. Even the elect may be deceived if we are not firmly grounded in God's Word and if we aren't walking in intimate fellowship with the living God. (See Mark 13:22–23.)

ARE YOU OPERATING IN THE ORDER OF NIMROD?

Nimrod was a type and shadow of the Antichrist. He manifested or revealed his rebellion in the form of a confederacy and an open revolt against God. Genesis 10:9 says Nimrod "was a mighty hunter before the LORD; therefore it is said, 'Like Nimrod the mighty hunter *before the LORD*'" (italics added). The next verse says Nimrod's kingdom began with Babel. In other words, Nimrod pushed his own order and might right in the face of God, and the people of God went with him. If we worship God in church on

Sundays, yet go along with the world's godless agenda for righting society's wrongs Monday through Saturday, then we are in the order of Nimrod and in direct rebellion against the order of God!

The path I've just described leads to some complications that Daniel accurately predicted when he related the description of this false leader many centuries ago. This isn't *my opinion;* it is God's Word:

> Then the king shall do according to his own will: he shall exalt and magnify himself above every god, shall speak blasphemies against the God of gods, and shall prosper till the wrath has been accomplished; for what has been determined shall be done. He shall regard neither the God of his fathers nor the desire of women, nor regard any god; for he shall exalt himself above them all.
>
> —DANIEL 11:36–37

Any leader inspired by Satan to lead a rebellion against God must also strike out at the foundation of God's order in the earth. It is no accident that the church is being pressured to come into agreement with powerful gay lobby groups or face the consequences. Every segment of governmental power, from the Congress to the executive branch to the Supreme Court, is being lobbied, pressured, and wooed to support the anti-Christ, anti-Bible gay rights cause. Hawaii has passed laws recognizing domestic partnerships for homosexuals, and corporations by the thousands are beginning to cave in to strong gay demands. It is all part of the satanic agenda to undermine the foundation of marriage and the home that God first instituted in the Book of Genesis.

TWO EXTREMES THAT DO NOT COME FROM GOD

Genesis 10:9 refers to Nimrod as "the mighty hunter I

believe that Nimrod hunted men, not animals. In the midst of a godly movement to call men back to their God-ordained roles as true men, protectors, and leaders in the home, there are two counterfeit movements in the world. One, sponsored primarily by the lesbian and women's rights movements, seeks to make men like women (or at least subservient to them). This group actively encourages men to step out of their leadership roles; it also strongly supports the abortion rights issue.

The second movement that largely dominates our culture and the media tells men they should cruelly dominate everything in their path with no fear, no responsibilities, and no consequences. This kind of hormone-driven macho manhood is what created the wrongs and the leadership void that produced the feminist movement in the first place! Neither extreme came from God.

My point is this: When mankind reaches the point where it says, "Come, let us build ourselves a city, and a tower whose top is in the heavens; let us make a name for ourselves...," as the people did in Genesis 11:4, then we can count on God coming to the city. Nimrod was guilty of the most blatant defiance of God. He absolutely refused to obey God's commands passed down through Noah from Adam. Nimrod's agenda defied God's command to be fruitful and multiply (God's order for marriage and the family) and to subdue the earth under God's authority. He wanted to do it *his* way, apart from God's rule. He wanted to make a name for himself.

My friend, *God has already given us a name,* and it is the name of Jesus. We can pray in His name and command legions of demons to flee. All we have to do is humble ourselves under His mighty hand, and He will exalt us in due season. Our world, our nation, our cities, and our churches are out of order; Daddy is about to step into the picture.

3

GOD IS VISITING THE CHURCH OF DISORDER

I'm tired of church, and so is God. I'm not tired of worshiping the Lord; I'm not tired of hearing and reading God's Word; I'm not tired of God's people; and I'm not tired of witnessing and ministering to the lost and hurting. What I'm tired of is the man-made, man-dominated, man-centered facade that is *posing* as the true church.

Jesus Himself defined the true church in the local sense when He said, "For where two or three are gathered together in My name, *I am there* in the midst of them" (Matt. 18:20, italics added). However, I've been in many church services where there just wasn't room or time allotted on the agenda for Jesus to be there or have His say.

I have a burning passion to see God right here—in the middle of us—when we gather in His name. Unfortunately, we face a big problem that we haven't whipped yet. A lot of people have said over the centuries that the devil keeps us from seeing God. Others claim that the atmosphere of our age keeps us separated from God's tangible presence. The real truth is that the greatest problem hindering us from seeing God isn't the devil or any other outside element. Our biggest problem is *us!* We have made the gospel so complicated with man-made rules, regulations, and hypocrisy that we have hindered a habitation from God.

The best we have seen at this point in church history is just a *visitation*. I thank God for that, but we need an overwhelming *habitation* of God. *The church has been her own worst enemy.* Our problem has been perpetuated by ignorance, disobedience, and selfishness that has only multiplied from generation to generation. Although we are the children of God, we are perishing because of our lack of wisdom.

There are a lot of hungry folk out there. I often go to Christian conventions and conferences and find myself preaching something from God's Word that is totally opposite from what everyone else is saying. I believe the church should have graduated long ago from the "bless me" kind of gospel. In the words of the apostle Paul:

> For though by this time you ought to be teachers, you need someone to teach you again the first principles of the oracles of God; and you have come to need milk and not solid food. For everyone who partakes only of milk is unskilled in the word of righteousness, for he is a babe. But solid food belongs to those who are of full age, that is, those who by reason of use have their senses exercised to discern both good and evil.
> —HEBREWS 5:12–14

TICKLING THE EARS OF THE NURSERY SAINTS

We should be pounding Satan's doors and mending

broken bodies and hearts, but we're too busy tickling the ears of the nursery saints. Yet everywhere I go, people are so receptive that I know they are hungry. These people have been hungering for meat for a long time, and for reasons unknown to me, their spiritual fathers and mothers aren't feeding them grown-up food.

The odd thing is that I find almost as many pastors and preachers showing the same hunger. It seems they have been laboring to serve God and His people for years, but they have been pressured to do things "the way they have always been done" or else, when deep down inside them they will tell you, "I hear a different sound." How do I know this? It isn't hard to figure out. It doesn't even take much spiritual discernment. These people give themselves away, because when they hear the truth, their mouths hang open and their eyes become bright with excitement or wet with tears. All they really want is truth.

This nation—and the whole world—is crying out for truth, but they are not finding it in the place we like to call "the church" (sometimes I wonder what God calls it since it bears so little resemblance to anything in His Word). As a result, the non-Christian world and many of the people attending our churches follow an ever-changing batch of nontruth and lies. Yet there is a call, a voice, an unspoken word that God is whispering into the innermost parts of people around the world. They can't tell you where it comes from or repeat it word for word, but whenever they hear somebody stand up and pro-claim it, they lift their heads and feel their hearts beat faster.

ONLY CERTAIN ONES HEAR THE CALL

I often mention the story of Noah when trying to explain this "different sound" in the earth. I'm convinced that when Noah loaded up the ark with animals, only certain animals heard the call. God instructed Noah to bring them in two by two, so when Noah went to the nearest pride of lions and called out, all of them didn't come at his command. Most of them glanced his way and then ignored him, but two of them heard the call of destiny and lifted their heads. Perhaps at that same moment all of the animals that were normally prey for the lions also answered that same call.

Normally, the different species would be fighting with, fleeing from, or eating one another as is normal in the order of the earth and the natural food chain. But this time a different order descended on that portion of the planet. There was peace between the species because they were all *in the order of God*. The future of each species was at stake. Everything flowed according to a higher order to achieve a higher purpose. This is an eternal characteristic of the order of God.

Today God has raised up certain men and women to proclaim a living word from God for this hour. Everywhere these anointed spokespersons go, they find people who *lift their heads,* even while engaged in the normal order of things, and say, "I know that voice. I've heard it before." Thousands are being drawn to the Master according to a higher order that often challenges the existing order of men. Let me be plain: The existing order that is being challenged most often is the order of man in the institution we have come to call the church. It is time to tear down the foundations of ignorance among God's people so that God is free to be God.

We have a dangerous habit of reading the Bible as if it is a children's storybook. Once you close the cover to a storybook, you go back into the real world. God's Word is *not* a storybook. It is God's sword, sharp and two-edged for a very good reason: *It cuts both ways.* Jesus gave us a warning because we need it, and it is time to open the Book again and hear the Word of the Lord:

[Jesus] answered and said to them, "Why do you

also transgress the commandment of God because of your tradition?...Thus you have made the commandment of God of no effect by your tradition. Hypocrites! Well did Isaiah prophesy about you, saying:

'These people draw near to Me with their mouth,
And honor Me with their lips,
But their heart is far from Me.
And in vain they worship Me,
Teaching as doctrines the commandments of men.'"
—MATTHEW 15:3, 6–9

ENTER THE ERA OF TOTAL CHANGE

Jesus warns us that our needless man-made traditions can nullify the Word of God! I am convinced that the Western world—and America in particular—has enjoyed what may have been the best forty-year period in the last two thousand years in terms of weather conditions, economic prosperity, and the absence of large-scale, intercontinental war. However, we are about to go into an era of total change. What was constant will no longer be constant.

I'm tired of preachers who fill pulpits but never prepare their people for anything except "sliding up to the dinner table for cookies and milk." Most Christians don't want to mature because maturity brings added responsibilities and new priorities. Many of our preachers have fostered the mentality that church is some place you visit to feel good and to hear somebody tell you that your troubles are going to be over. We don't hear widespread preaching about the responsibility that comes with the cross. We don't see the people of God taking up their cross and following Jesus Christ with the same sense of urgency and mission that we read about in the New Testament church. Why? Has the world's need for Jesus grown any less urgent in our day than it was two thousand years ago?

LET ME SEE WHAT YOUR GODS ARE GOING TO DO NOW!

I do hear a radical message rising up out of the kingdom of God from a small minority. More and more voices are crying, "Enough is enough!" It is clear to anyone with eyes to see and ears to hear that we are about to cross an invisible boundary into a state of major change and uncertainty. Over the last few decades our societal and governmental structures have placed their trust not in God, but in things such as computer data banks, the Federal Reserve, and the peace-keeping forces of the United Nations. At this writing we are about to go into the next millennium, and God is saying to our society, "All right, let Me see what your gods are going to do now."

The world isn't even prepared to deal with the Y2K (Year 2000) problem that may well shut down or disrupt most of the computers currently operating our fixed machinery, memory management systems, financial reports and analysis, military hardware, procurement, and mass transit and media systems. How can it solve the deeper problems?

The church is not prepared to go into the next millennium because we have too many people who are preaching the Rapture to God's people. Yet it is clear that this is *not* where God is moving right now. Yes, He is coming, but He is not coming to "rapture" or "snatch away" His scared and overcome people and then leave the planet in cinders. He is coming to *take over* and rule and reign with a bride, the true grown-up church, who has neither spot nor wrinkle. The fact is that we have a wonderful opportunity to rise up in God's glory right now because He is pulling down *everything* that has exalted itself against His Word.

SOME CHURCH FOLK ARE GOING TO BE OFFENDED BY GOD

It is no accident that the hidden sins of the White House, Congress, and many prominent churches and ministries have been brought into broad daylight over the last decade. Morality is part of it, but God is specifically targeting everything and everyone that have called themselves authorities, and He is shining His piercing light of glory on them. God is cleaning house, and the church is not making herself ready. It is my burning passion to see His face, but I am afraid that a lot of church folk are going to be very much offended by the way God is going to act. It will be even tougher for certain church leaders:

> Then His disciples came and said to Him, "Do You know that the Pharisees were offended when they heard this saying?"
>
> But He answered and said, "Every plant which My heavenly Father has not planted will be uprooted. Let them alone. They are blind leaders of the blind. And if the blind leads the blind, both will fall into a ditch."
>
> —MATTHEW 15:12–14

Judgment always *begins* in the house of God (1 Pet. 4:17). Right now He is separating the sheep from the goats just as Jesus described the separation of the nations in Matthew 25:32. He is about to raise up new leaders who have ears to hear the new sound of His Spirit. Somehow I don't think the leaders who are going to take us into the next millennium will be the same church leaders we had in the sixties, seventies, eighties, or even in the nineties. I've confessed to my congregation that I don't even know if I am strong enough to lead them where God has revealed that I should take them in the next millennium.

God is not looking for leaders who are searching for a pattern, because there is no pattern other than Jesus, the pattern Son. The Father is looking for people who have been totally broken and are dead to self and selfish ambitions. He is looking for "Joshua faith," not "Moses faith," in this new breed of leader. Moses was one of the greatest leaders in the Bible, but even Moses had to wait until the water was parted to cross the Red Sea. Joshua was required by the Lord to *step out* into the flood waters of uncertainty while trusting God to stop the river Jordan. (See Joshua 3:11–17.)

IT IS TIME TO CHALLENGE THE MISGUIDED TO HONOR GOD'S DECREES

God is searching for a people who will step out into the water just on a promise. This kind of church leader is in short supply today. We have allowed the government to tell us, "You can't pray in school; you can't talk about God," and slap our hands. Yet if we make the effort to talk to government officials and school administrators individually about the problems they face, we will find that many of them know they need God personally and in the schools. They know the nation needs God too, and they are actually looking for somebody to stand up and challenge the misguided "powers that be" who try to set aside the decrees of God.

While we, as part of the many-membered church, bicker and fight among ourselves over every minor point and opinion, we've failed to notice that God has left our fractured groups behind. We are on a mission, pressing on to fulfill our destiny in God's purpose. God Himself is saying, "Enough is enough. The fullness of time is now, and I am ready to reveal Myself as never before."

Sometime after the ministry of the original apostles, the church lost the point of evangelism; that error has produced generational weakness and spiritual infertility in the ranks of God's people. Again God says, "Enough is enough!"

WE HAD A BABY AND LEFT HIM AT THE ALTAR!

If we want a clear picture of the problem, let us look at the statistics of single-parent households in the United States. "How does that tie in to the church missing the point on evangelism, Bishop?" The two are linked at the heart.

God raised up powerful men's ministries like Dr. Edwin Louis Cole's Christian Men's Network, Promise Keepers, and Bishop T. D. Jakes's ManPower to restore true manhood to the church and the nation. Those ministries have run into opposition from feminists, but their goal is to put men back in their homes so they can be faithful husbands, loving fathers, and diligent mentors. The fact that we have an epidemic of men abandoning their wives and children speaks of a much deeper spiritual problem. I have a shocking statement to make: *The church did it first.*

The child abandonment epidemic happened in the spirit realm first. The church has pushed evangelism for more than one hundred years, and the central focus has been to get folks saved. There is only one problem with that. The Lord didn't say, "Go ye into all the world and get folks saved." He said, *"Make disciples."* The difference between the two is almost as significant as the difference between someone visiting your house and someone moving in permanently as a member of your family.

We refuse to mature the people we lead to Christ, but then we whine and wonder why they become Jehovah's Witnesses the next week, and the following year turn up on the street corner wearing the bow-tie and suit uniform of the Nation of Islam. The reason shouldn't be hard to figure out. We had a baby and left him at the altar so we could count our "growth numbers" to see if we beat the First Church down the road. Ministers will brag to one another in sanctimonious tones, "Oh, brother, I had a crusade last week, and do you know that we had five hundred get saved?" I rejoice over the souls, but I have to ask, *"What happened afterward?"*

I'M TIRED OF THUMB-SUCKERS AND OVERAGE BOTTLE-BABIES

Billy Graham was probably the only one I know of who really set up a system to take care of the thousands of spiritual babies he won to the Lord in various cities. He made sure they were contacted by a Bible-believing church that would care for the new believers and help them grow up and mature in Christ. Outside of this one notable exception, everyone else that I know just hopped on the big crusade bandwagon. For the most part, local churches, evangelists, and televangelists especially are guilty of conceiving and birthing spiritual babies, only to abandon them at the altar.

I believe God is orchestrating a major shift in leadership and ministry that will astound the minds of the experts. He is telling us, "You are going to either grow up or fall down—but I'm tired of thumb-suckers and overage bottle-babies in My church."

DON'T PERPETUATE WHAT GOD NEVER GAVE YOU

So, what has the church done about this? Our answer has been to schedule and attend more conventions about church growth and raise up more megachurches, all the while perpetuating things that God never ordained. I believe God is sick of it.

God isn't against megachurches per se. I pastor what many would call a megachurch, and I know God's favor and blessing is upon us. However, that is only because we had to learn some very painful lessons about God's order. We had to *change*. We had to allow some things to *die* that were never God's in the first place. We had to learn how to disciple and nurture new believers God's way when we had two thousand people before He would entrust us with eleven times that number. (We need to remember that the parable of the talents in Matthew 25:14–30 applies to local church congregations and ministers as well as to individuals in God's kingdom.)

The passion I have received from the Lord (and the passion that I want to impress upon you) is the passion to step into public and religious arenas at God's direction and put everything on the line by challenging ungodly systems that hold people in bondage. It is time for God's people to strip away the secrecy and openly take a stand.

> You are the light of the world. A city that is set on a hill cannot be hidden. Nor do they light a lamp and put it under a basket, but on a lampstand, and it gives light to all who are in the house. Let your light so shine before men, that they may see your good works and glorify your Father in heaven.
>
> —MATTHEW 5:14–16

We need to take the bushel basket off and boldly shine the light God gave us.

THE LION WILL COME TO TAKE OVER, NOT ROLL OVER

Perhaps God has sent the spirit of Elijah to modern John the Baptists in our generation to prepare again the way for the coming of the Lord. If that is the case, then we can be sure Jesus Christ won't come as a meek, sacrificial Lamb this time. He finished that mission more than two thousand years ago. This time He will come to take over this planet as the Lion of Judah, not roll over as the kitten of the kingdom. He is the King of kings and Lord of lords, and it is time for us to acknowledge it. God wants us to be unconventional enough to challenge the status quo in every place and every situation where it opposes the Word and will of God. That means we need to take our stand for truth in both the public marketplace and the church sanctuary.

I knew God was having His way in our church family and in my ministry when we started seeing people by the hundreds *relocate* to Atlanta from distant cities such as New York City and Chicago just because they heard that "sound" of God in our ministry. We don't pretend to be the only source of truth or anointing in God's kingdom; there are many more right in the city of Atlanta, as well as throughout North America and the world. But we have learned to take God's call and challenge seriously.

My heart aches for men who leave the major men's meetings each summer after having their hopes lifted up over a weekend, only to go home to near or total spiritual starvation. Although many men who attend events such as the Promise Keepers' conventions come from strong, Christ-centered churches who preach the truth from God's Word, some men are trapped in spiritually dead churches where the Holy Spirit is not welcome and God's Word is not preached. I pray that these men's meetings will continue as long as God blesses them, but I also know God said to me, "I want you to get this word out to the hungry. I want you to speak out and write down the things I have given you from My Word so others can receive them and take a bold stand for Me."

Nearly every month of the year, I meet hundreds of men who hear what I say and lift their heads to respond, but they are still stuck in sin or in a church system that honors man and man's traditions more than the living God. I want these men to hear the "different sound" of God's voice and be so challenged that they must step out of the bondage that binds them.

I've often had men tell me the same things after a meeting: "I'm glad to find out that I haven't lost my mind. I never thought I would hear somebody saying the same things that I am hearing God speak to my spirit! It is like a breath of fresh air. I said to myself, *There has to be somebody bold enough to say what I've been thinking.*"

SOME OF THIS STUFF WE'RE DOING ISN'T WORKING

When I minister at various Bible or church conventions, I often ask, "Aren't you sick of being delivered from the same thing six or seven times? How many meetings are you going to have to attend to find out that some of this stuff we're doing ain't working?" Time and again I discover that I said in public what a lot of people were thinking in secret, and it literally seems to galvanize their thinking and move them to concrete action. This is my mandate from God.

I want the church to act as if God is actually God. Too many times in too many churches, we act as if we can't actually let God run His church because He is so unpredictable. "Why, we might miss welcoming the visitors or something."

One of my dear friends and my spiritual father, Dr. Mark Hanby, once told me, "What would happen if God asked you, 'Why did you do those things I never told you to do?'" That comment had a deep impact on me, and I've discovered that it scares pastors. Why? Because they know that *if God never showed up,* their church services would still go on just fine without Him. What does that tell you about God's definition vs. man's definition of *church?* For the most part, God isn't showing up in most of America's churches.

WE HAVE PRESENTED A PERVERTED GOSPEL

The modern church has managed to present the gospel in such a perverted way that no one is really willing to die for it. This isn't the case in China, Pakistan, and countless other areas where persecution against Christians is the norm. Jesus preached the pure gospel of the kingdom. So did Peter, Stephen, and the apostle Paul. When they preached the gospel, people recognized the "different sound" and raised their heads, thinking, *I finally believe, and there's no other way. I've got to die for this. This is what I was born for.*

We have watered down the gospel to make it seeker-friendly. In doing so we have come into "agreement" with homosexuality, abortion, and countless other vital issues about which God's Word is clear; yet we choose to remain silent and do nothing. In God's eyes we are guilty of "aiding and abetting" when we remain silent while God says, "Speak!"

The church has failed to groom political leaders or do much of anything to impact her host cities. We're interested in having church and going home, therefore the commitment level of the saints is very low. When the Spirit of God says to our hearts, "Let's move out to the streets so we can meet needs. Let's feed the poor every weekend. Let's plant a church in the heart of the downtown area so we can bring God's light into the darkness," He gets the reply, "Yeah, let's do that. I'll do it *if I can just stay in my culture.*"

We lack the tenacity that many of our forefathers had when they braved public persecution or imprisonment to stand for what they believed from God's Word. Today most people look at the gospel of Jesus Christ as "optional equipment"—just another thing that makes society better. We ministers have to take some of the blame for that because a lot of the problem is in the presentation. (I have repented to my congregation for my sermons during my first few years of service.)

I believe God is angry with us. He said through the prophet Isaiah:

For My name's sake I will defer My anger,

And for My praise I will restrain it from you,
So that I do not cut you off.
Behold, I have refined you, but not as silver;
I have tested you in the furnace of affliction.
For My own sake, for My own sake, I will do it;
For how should My name be profaned?
And I will not give My glory to another.

—Isaiah 48:9–11

God said, "I'm going to do all of this for you in the midst of your disobedience, but it is only because you have misrepresented the kingdom. If I did with you what I want to do with you, people would say I wasn't God. Now I have to show up to prove to everybody else I AM God."

I recently looked into the television cameras that beam our ministry to the nation and around the world and said, "In a lot of the churches God is only showing up because of His name. His name is at stake because we've misrepresented it; if He didn't show up, people wouldn't believe He was God."

God shouldn't have to show up in our churches just to defend Himself due to our misrepresentation. That is the way of the "church of disorder." We should be so dedicated and willing to serve Him that He shows up *just because He's pleased*.

THE NEW ORDER
OF GOD

One of the most life-changing things that God ever did to me happened about four years ago. That was the day I became *pastor.* Up until that time I was the hired preacher who was called the pastor. I had a deacon board gripping the purse strings (controlling the money) and carefully guarding its authority over me in the name of protecting the sheep. These men were not evil; they were basically good men operating outside of God's order.

When I first came to New Birth Missionary Baptist Church in Atlanta, the church had about three hundred people and a ruling board that signed the checks and expected to tell the man of God when to jump and how high. I struggled along trying to obey God under this system for almost seven years before I finally took a stand; by that time New Birth had grown to a congregation of about two thousand people.

I remember wanting to hire a music director to help

carry the load in our growing church, but the leadership vetoed my request without another thought. The Baptist board system was the only form of church government I had ever known outside of my theological training, but God began to re-educate me and reform my thinking to match what *His Word* says about local church government.

This church had split off from other congregations twice in its history, so I knew that a spirit of schism or division was operating in it or upon it in some way. Even though the Lord began to show me how to separate His way from man's way of governing the church, I knew I had to be wise and patient. If I had used the Bible to "set those men straight," the local church body would have split again *because some leaders had more power in that church than the Word of God did.* The congregation was just too immature in the Word at that time to handle such a confrontation.

I had attended some of meetings that Tony Evans held, and I was deeply impressed by the Lord when I heard Dr. Evans talk about the authority of Scripture. I was also encouraged and built up during the many hours I spent talking with two godly men who still speak into my life with great authority and faithfulness. Bishop T. D. Jakes was a faithful brother, mentor, and spiritual father (although he is actually younger than I am), and he pledged to stand with me when the time came. My other wise counselor was Dr. Mark Hanby, a man recognized around the world for his integrity and wisdom in matters of church government, relationships, and kingdom purposes.

GOD SAID, "I HAVE NOTHING TO DO WITH MOST CHURCHES"

God spoke to me over a period of time and confirmed the convictions I'd formed about divine order through my study and meditation in God's Word. I knew the time had come for a change, but I also sensed that what I did and how I did it would become a foundation for things yet to come in my life. God said to me, "If you put this church in My order, I will take it. It will be Mine." I asked for more understanding about His order, and the Lord spoke definitely and specifically to my spirit about one of the most dangerous conditions existing in the church:

> I have nothing to do with most of the churches in America because they are run by constitutions that "protect" them from the "set ministry" I have placed in their midst to lead them. They have replaced My order with their own rules and regulations, and they have chosen to direct their own destiny by "vote" instead of by My Spirit and My revealed Word.

Once I heard from the Lord, I knew what I had to do. Week after week I taught the congregation the revelations I'd received about the divine authority of Scripture and the order of God in our lives, our homes, and the church. While I labored to build up the congregation in God's Word every Sunday, many of the leaders labored to tear me down in private meetings behind closed doors.

Many times God prompted me to do important things so New Birth could enter its destiny as a church. Yet time and again the leadership would outvote both me and the Lord who gave me the dream to reach out or begin a new ministry. There were many nights when I would go home and just weep, but I would never let the congregation know. I would always give the best for my leaders publicly, but the truth is that they had my hands tied. I refused to speak evil of these men from the pulpit or in private; I simply left the matter in God's hands. That was the wisest thing I could ever have done.

WE ARE OUT OF THE WILL OF GOD

At the conclusion of the twelfth message in the series on the authority of God's Word and the proper order of

God's house, I stood up and asked the congregation (with many of the board members and leaders opposed to me at the front), "Do you believe the Word of God is true?" Everyone shouted, "Yeah!"

Every eye followed my movements as I held up a copy of the church constitution in one hand and my Bible in the other. "We are out of the will of God," I declared, "and I'm asking the deacons, the trustees, the elders, and the ministers to look at this constitution and this Bible. Then whatever is not biblical in this constitution, *take it out*." The congregation immediately applauded because that is what they wanted. They had heard the Word of God for themselves, and they wanted the blessings that come with God's order. (Some of the board members also felt the same way.)

When the applause died down, I recited to the congregation the word God had given to me about His order, and I will repeat it again because it is just that important:

> I have nothing to do with most of the churches in America because they are run by constitutions that "protect" them from the "set ministry" I have placed in their midst to lead them. They have replaced My order with their own rules and regulations, and they have chosen to direct their own destiny by "vote" instead of by My Spirit and My revealed Word.

I didn't show up for any of those constitutional meetings except the last one because the Lord told me not to. I told the church leadership, "I'm not going to make this personal. In fact, I'm not even going to show up." I said it because some of the leaders had said to me, "Well, you're just trying to get full control." So I didn't show up; I just left them alone with the Bible and their constitution that contained so little of God's Word.

1. *In Our Own Words,* compiled by Eliza Dinwiddie-Boyd (New York: Avon Books, 1996), p. 73.

When the leaders looked at the Scriptures and compared them with what was written in the church constitution, they discovered there was very little that they could keep. Yet they knew they couldn't come back to me and not change the constitution, because I went back to the congregation and said, *"Here is what the Scripture says,* and here is what the church leadership is saying we have to keep."

Not only was I instructed about the *need* for change in the order of God's house at New Birth, but God also told me *how* to bring about that change His way. I followed the Lord's direction and found myself totally off the hook. I had quietly labored and preached the Word, while a few people beat me up in private rooms away from every eye—or so they thought. But there is One who sees all things and keeps an account of every word said and every deed done.

The day I stood up and challenged the church leadership to come into God's order, something supernatural happened at New Birth. The people in the congregation matured in their understanding of and loyalty to God's Word. They reached the point where they would no longer rely on human personality, but on the person of Christ. Their main point of reference had shifted from the opinions of men to God's Word. Once I told them what God had said to me about taking back the church as His own, things started to happen.

BISHOP JAKES SAID SOME THINGS, AND WE HAD CHURCH!

Just as he had promised, Bishop T. D. Jakes flew into Atlanta to stand by my side the following Sunday. I felt like a little boy standing beside Bishop Jakes, and he kept telling me, "Everything's gonna be all right, son." On the one hand I knew I had obeyed the Lord by challenging the ungodly governmental structure at New Birth, but on the other hand the church board did have the legal right under the existing church constitution to vote me out.

As I stood up before the congregation that day, I didn't know whether or not I would be preaching there after that service. I did know this much: I had obeyed God, and that was what mattered to me the most in that moment. I introduced Bishop Jakes to the people. He made a few remarks, and then *we had church!* I became the true pastor of New Birth Missionary Baptist Church that day, and things exploded from that day on.

Although most of the former leaders have gone on to other churches, a few remained at New Birth, and they have been totally transformed. They tell me they are being blessed more now than ever before in their lives and ministries; they don't even understand now why they held on to the old system as long as they did. Because of their willingness to change and be open to God, they serve as true examples of the journey that we must take in order to survive in this transitional time. They also serve as spiritual role models for me whenever I am faced with, or find myself fighting, major changes that God places before me in my own life.

Everything turned around at New Birth when we made up our minds to set our house in order God's way. The house of God, the church, is seriously out of order today. This outlaw order can be found at the highest levels of church leadership, but it is also woven into every area of our individual and family lives.

I believe that the destiny of entire local church bodies depends on their willingness to hear this word (from me or from any other godly source) and act on it. This is a very tough word, but I offer no apologies. It is a tough word for men, and it is a liberating word today for women. It is a word of hope for the children and a word of destiny for the family. It is a word of power for the church in an age of confrontation with the powers of darkness. An old Ghanian proverb from the tribe of Ashanti states that *the ruin of a nation begins in the homes of its people.*[1]

The cancer doesn't begin in the
Congress. Why not? The people in
people who voted them into those
homes. No matter what problem y
you point out, I guarantee you it
somehow, some way. Where we a
we are as a church was birthed i

ARE YOU STILL WORKING THROUGH THE PAIN OF YESTERDAY?

I'll never forget the character named Jenny in the movie *Forrest Gump.* The central character, Forrest Gump, was a man who overcame many obstacles to live a wonderful life. Jenny was Forrest's closest childhood friend and his only true love all his life. Yet very few people really remember Jenny's character because they were so keyed in on Forrest. Jenny came from a home of abuse. She was abused by her father, and by the time she was able to run away from home, most of the damage to her life had already been done.

If you focus in on Jenny's character, you will see that throughout the rest of the movie, she was trying to work herself out of the pain she endured in her childhood home. Jenny went from abusive relationship to abusive relationship; she was involved in drugs and everything else that came along as she tried to find herself. This pattern of compulsive self-destruction continued until she died an early death after contracting AIDS.

Many of us left home a long time ago, but we are still working through the pain we endured there. We've been praying for deliverance from the hang-ups, the verbal and mental abuse, the physical and sexual abuse, the chronic poverty, or the lack of encouragement and love. All of these things can be traced directly back to our earliest days in the *home.*

It is in the *home* that Satan plants time bombs in your

only show up after you say, "I do." These im-
bombs from your parents' unhappy marriage,
fractured personalities, or a relative's twisted sexual
petites will explode with virtually no warning and
threaten the very fabric of your own marriage two or
three decades later. (This is why it is so important for
single Christians thinking of marriage to pray to the Lord,
"Search me, O God, and if You find anything that is not
clean, not right, or not good, help me remove it. Heal me,
O Lord." Before you say "I do," get those hidden things
revealed and worked out of your life with God's help.)

Order in a family is important because each generation
is to go on to a new and greater glory than the previous
generation. God intends for each new generation to build
on the foundation and successes of the last generation.
That is the reason why God passes on everything through
a man. If you follow the lineage of Abraham, Isaac, and
Jacob, you will see that the lineage is always being
passed on and going *higher*. But the problem is that we
stop passing on our successes through lack of order. We
poison our seed and doom them to start over.

LIVING ON YESTERDAY'S SEEDS AND DEEDS

The American church essentially died around 1950, especially in the Black community. That is when we decided
to stop advancing and instead live on yesterday's seeds
and deeds. We started doing the same old thing while
avoiding anything new in God. So here we are, still con-
ducting 1955-vintage spiritual warfare, while the devil has
advanced to a new millennium. He is waging state-of-the-
art warfare against a church that hasn't left the 1950s!

It is all because there is no order in the house. We are
not shooting our children out like arrows of God into the
future. We haven't equipped them with our anointing,
our knowledge, and their full godly inheritance.

My son Kody is supposed to do even greater things

than I have done. I am supposed to build a platform upon which he will rise up and do even greater exploits. But if I poison him *in the house,* he will not be able to do them. Instead, he will spend most of his life finding out who he is and undoing the evil I did to him in his early years. Now do you see why God's order is so important in the house?

It all begins with man. In the Book of Genesis God established the man as the foundation for both the family and the church:

> This is the history of the heavens and the earth when they were created, in the day that the LORD God made the earth and the heavens, before any plant of the field was in the earth and before any herb of the field had grown. For the LORD God had not caused it to rain on the earth, and there was no man to till the ground.
> —GENESIS 2:4–5

God needed a man. There was mist to maintain the proper moisture, but there was no rain and no man to move forward. God needed man.

WHATEVER GOD PUTS FIRST IS A FOUNDATION

Genesis 2:7 says, "And the LORD God formed man of the dust of the ground, and breathed into his nostrils the breath of life; and man became a living being." Whatever God wants, He gets; God doesn't do anything haphazardly or by accident. The first earthly being God created was a man. He made man first, and whatever He puts first is a foundation.

Any foundation must be strong enough to handle the structure that will be built on it afterward. (That means that God has rested the family, the community, the church, and the nation on man.) Then came Eve, and after that came the children in due order. God has rested everything on man. When you want to find out what the problems are in the community or in the nation, you will end up where God started—with man. If you want to fix the problems, you start with man and work your way back.

Every man reading these words is under pressure and stress. If you are at the breaking point, I can assure you that the only reason you are about to break is because somewhere, in some way, you are not doing things the way God has ordained. It sounds tough and unfair, but the fact is that you are a foundation. Therefore, since God doesn't make mistakes, you as the foundation that God laid down can support and shoulder whatever burden God allows to be laid on you. He will give you the grace and strength to handle *everything He has ordained*.

ARE YOU DOING SOMETHING GOD NEVER TOLD YOU TO DO?

However, if you take on something God never told you to do, or if you decide to do something your way instead of His way, then you are in danger of breaking under a load that isn't yours. God didn't make man the foundation because men are superior to women; they are not. He made man the foundation because He wanted to, and He never expected men to stand in their human strength. God expects men to stand on the spiritual strength of the Rock of salvation, the Son of God.

Women have an equally high calling, value, and anointing from God. Yet in God's order their chief function in the home, in life, and in the marriage relationship is different from man's function. God went to the ground to make man, but He went to the man to make woman.

Have you ever noticed that men generally look attractive even when they are dirty? Even the well-researched and expensive commercials on television have no problem showing a man who is sweaty and dirty on the job getting flirty glances from a well-dressed woman. Women, for some reason, just don't look attractive when they are dirty. That is because the woman wasn't pulled out of the ground; she was pulled out of man.

God covered man, pulled the woman out of man, and took the child out of the woman. Now He expects the man to cover the woman and the child. Whatever God took out of man and put in woman, He never put back. That is why we continue to seek each other out to find what we don't have.

Man and woman are divided in function but equal in essence. God made the woman to be a wife and a mother. Her body is uniquely equipped with a womb, with breasts, and with the bone structure and complex hormonal systems necessary to conceive, carry, bear, and nurture children.

The medical profession decided they knew better than God in the 1950s and 1960s when they announced that it was old-fashioned and second-best for new mothers to nurse their babies. But God's way has finally prevailed, and the natural way of nursing babies is back. Although I am thankful for baby formula in cases where nursing is impossible or difficult at best, the use of formula was pushed as a way that was better than God's way.

ISRAELITE MOTHERS NURSED BABIES
FOR FIVE YEARS

If you study women and motherhood in biblical times, you will see that it was customary for mothers to nurse their children for the first five years of their lives—at first as the baby's sole source of nutrition, and later on as a key supplement to solid food in the diet. They had children who were obedient because they were kept close to nurture and train. Although the children also received direct input from grandparents and other adult family members, they weren't put in the care of strangers. Not only did mothers feed them physically, but they also fed them spiritually and emotionally. As the children grew older, they were able to stand on a good foundation.

Even unsaved psychologists say that the basic personality of a human being is formed in the *first five years* of life. The pediatric profession has acknowledged that babies who are nursed by their mothers have fewer childhood infections and are more secure and well-adjusted emotionally and socially in later years. Though I'm not pressuring mothers to nurse their children for five years, God has ordained that nurturing mothers form an essential foundation in little boys and girls that they will need to help them fulfill their destinies in life.

Fathers, however, give their children purpose and identity. Experts tell us that boys get their identities from their fathers. Girls also form their identities based on their fathers' affirmation (or lack thereof). It starts with both parents operating in their roles in the home.

Psalm 127:1 says, "Unless the Lord builds the house, they labor in vain who build it." The psalmist goes on to say:

> Behold, children are a heritage from the LORD,
> The fruit of the womb is a reward.
> Like arrows in the hand of a warrior,
> So are the children of one's youth.
> Happy is the man who has his quiver full of them;
> They shall not be ashamed,
> But shall speak with their enemies in the gate.
> —PSALM 127:3–5

WE ABORT OUR FUTURE THROUGH PRESENT-DAY IGNORANCE

Children are God's arrows in our hands, and it is our responsibility and privilege to launch them into the future equipped with all of the accumulated knowledge, wisdom, wealth, and power we have gained and that our forefathers have left us. Our problem is that we are constantly aborting our future generations through present-day ignorance and disorder.

I am the son of a preacher, but the only reason I am here is because my mother understood the Scriptures and had the strength of conviction and character to submit to my father—even when he didn't deserve it. When she married him, he hid two secrets from her: He was an alcoholic, and he really wasn't saved. Mom discovered the truth after she married Dad, but because she was married to him, she submitted to him and respected him anyway.

Mom would get up in the morning and cook breakfast from scratch—the old-fashioned way. If Daddy came home at eleven o'clock or midnight (even without a phone call, and sometimes with some very shaky reasons), she would get out of bed and fix him a plate of food. Then she would sit there until he was finished, wash the dishes, and have his clothes ready for the next day.

If it wasn't for Mom, I wouldn't be where I am today. You see, Daddy wouldn't go to church with her on Sunday mornings. She never told me this (for obvious reasons), but as a grown man today, I am sure that Mom would wake up on Sunday mornings and "minister" to Dad before she got out of bed as only a wife can. (This could serve as an invaluable lesson to women who say, "My unsaved husband won't let me go to church." Take a lesson from my godly mother—you minister to your husband first, then get up and cook for him. He'll end up going to church *with you*.) Only then would she leave and take me to church with her. I believe the reason my daddy let her go to church in those days was because Mom was careful to take care of him before she left.

Daddy did not believe in Jesus Christ, and he was an alcoholic who got mean when he was drunk. Mom still served him and respected him. Mom told me that after a while, my daddy would get up and kind of peer out between the window curtains when she left for church. (Again, I am thoroughly convinced it was because my mother did "ministry" before she left.)

My mom is a fine woman in the best sense of the word,

and she told me, "Honey, when I would get ready to go to church in the early days, I'd put my nice stockings on, and I'd get a nice dress to wear—even if it meant I had to work all week just to pay for it. I made sure I looked the best I could, and I'd spray on a little perfume before I walked past Daddy to go to church. At first he wouldn't pay any attention to me. But about a year later, I'd catch him kind of peeping at me out of the corner of his eye as I was getting ready to go."

She said that two years later, Daddy wasn't pretending anymore. He would sit up on the side of the bed and watch her when she left the house for church. Three years later, Mom made it even tougher. "I would walk to church just because I wanted him to get a 'good view' as I was leaving. I had a way of walking so that he just couldn't stand it. I would see him peeping around the door to see me go. One morning I took good care of him (Mom purposely didn't fill in the details), and I fixed his breakfast. Then I told him, 'I am going to church, Honey.'"

When she looked around, Daddy was dressed. Then he took her by the arm and said, "I am going with you." That day the pastor preached a mighty sermon, and my daddy got up, stepped past my mama in the pew, and walked down the aisle. Not only did he get saved that day, but he received a call to the ministry, too. Daddy not only answered the call to the ministry, but he also started many churches. Listen to me: Daddy did that because a woman was able to respect him enough to know that God had a call on him—even before he knew it himself.

I WAS AN ARROW SHOT INTO THE NEXT GENERATION

My daddy's call was to start churches. I never remember Daddy pastoring one church for more than three years. He would go in and pioneer a church, build a nice building, and then leave. Guess what? That same pioneering legacy is going on today in my ministry, but to an even greater degree. I was an arrow that was shot into the next generation. God is bringing pastors to me from all over this country who are laying down their ordination certificates and saying, "I am submitting to you, Bishop, and I am bringing my church under the authority of this church." I tell you that this leadership mantle and calling was birthed first in my daddy, the called-out builder of churches. In my generation, God is submitting under this authority churches that are already built.

It wasn't easy for my mother to submit to and respect my alcoholic father in the early days, but she had an unshakable conviction that God's Word was true, and she lived according to her conviction. I thank God that my mother was a godly woman with the faith to stand when everything around her told her to run.

I can remember the day that she almost left. She had just about had enough, and she started packing her things. I was crying my heart out in the bathroom, and finally I went to her because I knew my daddy was being a stubborn fool. I said, "Mama, if you leave, I'll die." And she said, "I ain't going nowhere." Because my godly mother was willing to cover me, I'm here fulfilling my divine call today.

WE'RE FIGHTING THE BATTLE AND LOSING THE WAR

Whether male or female we need to understand that all of the problems we fill our days with—marital, child-rearing, financial, and relational—are distractions and smoke screens that the devil is using to keep our eyes off what God has ordained for us to do. We as members of the body of Christ have been drawn away to little battles in our backyards, but we are losing the fight to fulfill our divine destinies in God. We are fighting the battles of our own choosing, not realizing we are passing up a far greater treasure by losing the war of obedience to God's will and Word.

One of our most serious problems is that we have trained the congregations in the body of Christ to be spiritually selfish. We come to church services with the primary goal of enjoying ourselves and being blessed. It is good to be blessed, but God has a higher purpose and priority for our lives than to be blessing-seekers all of our days. Our inward focus on personal blessings for "us four and no more" has caused us to miss what God is doing in the earth today. We are not saying to the Lord, "Your will be done." We are saying, "*My* will be done, and with as little trouble as possible please, Lord." We don't understand that *the only reason God blesses us is so that we can be a blessing!*

The Bible doesn't tell us, "Present your requests to God so you can avoid all sacrifice, which is unreasonable service anyway." No, the apostle Paul tells us, "I beseech you therefore, brethren, by the mercies of God, that you present your bodies a living sacrifice, holy, acceptable to God, which is your reasonable service" (Rom. 12:1).

THE ONE-STEP METHOD TO PERFECTION NOBODY WANTS

Many sincere Christians claim they are "suffering for Christ," but most of our "suffering" comes in one of two ways. We "suffer" because of our uncontrolled flesh, our desires, or our lack of discipline. We also "suffer" when we are in the middle of God's maturation process and are being conformed to Christ's image. The first kind of suffering isn't suffering at all; it is a warning to shape up, make right choices, and tell the flesh no. The second kind of suffering is actually the mercy of God at work in us. If we allow patience to have "its perfect work," as in the words of the apostle James, we will "be perfect and complete, lacking nothing" (James 1:4).

According to Ephesians 6, a fight is going on that we do not understand or even perceive in many cases. God wants to manifest His power through the church in this fight, and that is why it is so important for the church to get in the order of God. God's order strengthens the church and everything it touches. As the families are strengthened, the local church is strengthened, and the power of God can be manifested through the corporate body.

When I taught the series of messages on "Setting the House in Order," I took the people into the Book of Genesis to discover how God established His order in the *beginning*. Then we looked at God's order from the other side of the cross in Ephesians 5. These powerful books give us God's divine order for men, for women, for the family, for the saints, for motherhood, and for parenting, along with key instructions for submission to one another in our relationships.

We are a body of many different members united under one Head. It is vital that we find our place and function without envy or strife so we can all receive God's blessing and fulfill our destiny. If you have ever stubbed your little toe or broken a finger, you know how your whole body is affected when even one of your smallest and least noticed members is hurt or out of place. Things get even more serious when major organs or weight-bearing parts are out of place or missing.

YOU CAN TRACE EVERY PROBLEM TO THE MAN OF THE HOUSE

I believe you can trace every major problem affecting the church and society today to the man of the house. When the man shirks his God-given responsibilities in relationships, marriage, or the home, all hell breaks loose. Something else will quickly step in to fill the void a man's absence creates. Once the man steps back into God's order, everything else gets stronger.

You bring the measure of God's power that is manifested in your home to the local church. When you have nothing at home, you bring all of that nothingness to the church. So Christians are disappointed when they bring all of their nothingness together and expect something big to happen.

Why is it that nine out of every ten churches in this country don't even impact the single block of property their building occupies? They are out of the *order* of God; therefore the *power* of God is missing from the homes and lives of their people, individually and corporately. We can never have God's power unless we come into agreement with one another and come into God's order at home and at church.

When we come together in God's order under the influence of the same indwelling Spirit of God, we will see the kingdom of God *take over* through a manifestation of the power of God on a level we have never seen before. On the other hand, the churches that manage to have a wonderful time *without* the Spirit of God on Sundays and Wednesdays get only what they can produce in the flesh. Any church that operates outside of God's order is functioning in man's power; it has no power to influence and impact the world around it. This kind of church will find itself *overcome* by a society like the one described by the apostle Paul in his second letter to Timothy:

> But know this, that in the last days perilous times will come: For men will be lovers of themselves, lovers of money, boasters, proud, blasphemers, disobedient to parents, unthankful, unholy, unloving, unforgiving, slanderers, without self-control, brutal, despisers of good, traitors, headstrong, haughty, lovers of pleasure rather than lovers of God, having a form of godliness but denying its power. And from such people turn away!
>
> —2 TIMOTHY 3:1–5

This sounds like the news stories we hear year after

year describing the stars in the typical professional sports draft, doesn't it? This could be the personal biography of America's favorite musicians and movie stars, or even worse, a description of the elders' kids in your own church! What is happening to us? A quick survey tells us we have skyrocketing preteen pregnancies, free condom distribution in public schools, drive-by shootings, child pornography in print and on the Internet, abortion on demand, and do-it-yourself suicide machines. We also have rampant child abuse, near-total family breakdown, and murder without a second thought (especially if the killer is under the age of sixteen).

Judges 17:6 says, "In those days there was no king in Israel; *everyone did what was right in his own eyes*" (italics added). This plague has moved into the church. For instance, the leadership that was at New Birth when I arrived openly disregarded the ministry gift God had *set* in the body according to Ephesians 4:11–14 until God changed the order of things. Anytime we choose to "do what [is] right in [our] own eyes" *regardless of what the Scriptures say,* we have committed a sin that can poison every area of our lives.

GOD'S ORDER BRINGS BENEFITS AND BLESSING

The very year I obeyed God and the church adopted God's order instead of man's, the New Birth church family became debt free. God made one hundred seventy acres of prime property available to us adjacent to the Atlanta airport. The land was worth over ten million dollars, but the man who owned it was mad at his son, so he offered it to us for three million dollars.

I went to the bank and said, "We need three million dollars." The bankers looked at me and said, "Sir, we don't make those kinds of loans." I just smiled and said, "You'll make it. Just call me." The next day they called me, and we bought the land.

We held the property for fourteen months; then we sold it for fourteen million dollars, clearing eleven million dollars on the transaction after paying off our loan. We bought two hundred forty acres just up the street from our present location, paid off all of our bills, and put two million dollars in the bank. God did all of that, and we didn't even touch any of our tithes and offerings.

We have a fitness club and a five-acre park, and a tennis court was given to us. God has given us incredible favor— even our families will tell you that they have been blessed ever since we put our house in order.

That is the challenge the church in America faces in this hour. Once we get our houses, individually and corporately, in God's order, He will bless us. Once God's blessing comes, He expects us to stretch beyond our own abilities and resources to *do something* for Him where His glory is really needed.

God wants suburban churches to stretch themselves by faith at His direction to sow buildings, land, resources, and *people* in inner-city neighborhoods in Jesus' name. He wants big city churches to expand their vision and plant churches in rural areas where God's Word is hard to find. God wants to tear down every fence we have labored to build in the flesh over the last two centuries in America. He wants His church to take the lead by manifesting His glory in interracial reconciliation around the cross of Jesus. He wants the church to *take over* neighborhoods currently overtaken by crime, gang warfare, and ruling poverty spirits. These things will happen only when the church receives the new order of God and we get busy setting the house in order.

5

JUBILEE BEGINS WITH ATONEMENT

In 1998 the nation of Israel celebrated its first Year of Jubilee since the day Jesus Christ was crucified on a Roman cross in Jerusalem nearly two thousand years ago. God confirmed to many church leaders and congregations, including New Birth, that this was a great Jubilee year for the church as well as for Israel and the Jewish people.

The Jewish Year of Jubilee was ordained by God in Leviticus 25. God told the Jews to set aside the seventh day of every week as a Sabbath, a day of rest for man and worship to the Lord. Every seventh year was also set aside as a Sabbath year when the land would rest and God would supply the needs of the people by using the harvests of the previous six years.

Finally, the year after the seventh Sabbath year (the year after the forty-ninth year) was set aside as a Jubilee year. This was to be an extra fallow (nonworking) year for the land, and all land reverted back to its original owner. Jews who had been forced by poverty or circumstance to sell their property or sell themselves into slavery in order to pay debts were officially released. Their lands were redeemed by their near kinsmen or released by the most recent owners. This Jubilee reminded the people that all land belongs to the Lord, and it kept the wealthy from amassing so much land that the less fortunate would be forever placed under bondage.

I want to clarify something else about Jubilee before we look at the Book of Leviticus. In reality, there is no Hebrew word or term for Jubilee. The Hebrew term in the Scriptures is *yobel,* and it comes from a root word that means "to flow." It refers to a continuous trumpet blast used to signal the beginning of something of great importance and joy. I believe in my spirit that God did not allow the Jewish people to coin a specific Hebrew word to describe the Year of Jubilee because it is holy just as He is holy. In other words, all we have is the word describing how the Year of Jubilee was announced in Israel (with the blast of silver trumpets) and how men reacted to the joyful news. The event itself had no name.

God is always moving, so those who follow Him must also be ready to move, respond, and change at His command. I believe God purposely left it to us to discern the current meaning of Jubilee in our generation by seeing whatever He is doing among us and in us at the time. Jubilee is the arrival of God our Savior and Deliverer in the midst of every area of bondage, limitation, lack, or failure we may have. When the King of glory arrives on the scene, every form and fashion of darkness must flee. Even the darkest of situations takes on a whole new look in the light of His presence.

Jubilee is obviously more than a one-year event for those who have been redeemed by the blood of the Lamb; it is an unbroken state of grace in Jesus. However, the Lord brought some correction into my life after New Birth began to observe the Year of Jubilee in January of

1998. I went before my congregation many months later and told them that I had missed something important, and God wanted me to correct some things in *the house* concerning the full meaning of Jubilee.

Jubilee is a two-edged sabbath of God. Not only are you and I released from areas of bondage and lack in our lives, but we are required to do some releasing of our own! Not only do we have many lost things restored to us, but there is some restoration God expects us to do as well. Jubilee always begins with atonement.

> And you shall count seven sabbaths of years for yourself, seven times seven years; and the time of the seven sabbaths of years shall be to you forty-nine years. Then you shall cause the trumpet of the Jubilee to sound on the tenth day of the seventh month; on the Day of Atonement you shall make the trumpet to sound throughout all your land. And you shall consecrate the fiftieth year, and proclaim liberty throughout all the land to all its inhabitants. It shall be a Jubilee for you; and each of you shall return to his possession, and each of you shall return to his family.
> —LEVITICUS 25:8–10

Before Jesus Christ took away the sins of the world through His own sacrifice on the cross, the nation of Israel gathered once a year "on the tenth day of the seventh month" for a special day of confession and atonement (at-oneness) for sin. This was the only time in the whole year that the high priest of Israel could enter the holy of holies to make offerings for the sins of Israel. Unlike all the other feast days in Israel, the Day of Atonement was not marked by joy. It was a time for everyone to humble themselves before God and search their hearts for sin, disobedience, and offenses against God and man. It was a day of atoning *sacrifice,* marked by death of an innocent sacrifice to pay for the sins of a guilty people.

As Christians we remember the supreme *sacrifice* Jesus Christ made to bring us back to our heavenly Father and restore and redeem us to our inheritance in God. This is what God spoke to me by way of correction:

> I have ordained that in this season of Jubilee, My people must *first* make the sacrifices necessary to release My people. Only then will My Spirit be released to do everything I have ordained concerning you. Then the joy of Jubilee will come in its fullness.

No, I'm not saying that what Jesus accomplished on the cross wasn't enough to save and redeem us. I am saying that God isn't satisfied with a one-time repentance from sin. You and I sin everyday. We get angry at one another, and sometimes we hold grudges for decades because of our pride or prejudice. Jubilee in this generation means more than debt cancellation or financial freedom. It requires *sacrifice from you*. First you do what it takes to set others free; then you will be set free as well.

God is sick of traditional religious form and fashion because we usually use it to hide or mask the truth. This Jubilee will require *sacrifice,* not the rubbing of some kind of magical Bible or the recitation of some biblical mantra. Reread Leviticus 25:8–10 and ask yourself, "What happens during Jubilee?"

Jubilee involves a whole lot more than the canceling of debt. So many of us get so focused on the debt cancellation that if there *were* a Hebrew word for "Jubilee," we would tie it in to something about finances and permanently limit its meaning to one area of life. God never intended for debt cancellation to be the only connotation in the spirit realm for the Year of Jubilee.

We know from the Scriptures that Jubilee also involved the restoration or returning of all land to its original owners. Jubilee reminds us that God—not man—owns all the land on this planet. He is the one who made it, and He is the one who distributes it as He sees fit. It doesn't matter how much money we have or don't have; the land is God's, and He makes sure it gets into the hands of the people He chooses—without apology or explanation. When the land of a person or a family was in the hands of others, particularly non-Jewish owners, the nearest kinsman was obligated to purchase back (at his own expense) the land and restore it to his family member. This is what Boaz did for Ruth and Naomi. (See Ruth 3–4.)

Jubilee is a time when the enslaved are set free. This was especially true for Jews who had become indentured servants to other Jews to pay their debts. For every Jewish slave who was freed, there was also a Jewish slaveholder who was obligated to give up and release that Jewish slave. When a Jewish man was enslaved to a non-Jewish master, the man's nearest kinsman was obligated to pay his ransom and restore him to his family.

The Year of Jubilee is also meant to be a time when families who have been separated due to financial difficulties, enslavement, or war come back together. I want you to grasp this: God is saying that for the church, Jubilee means that relationships are healed.

It is time for the redeemed of the Lord, the near-kinsmen of the brethren, to relieve and take the burden off their brethren through the cancellation of debt, grievance, bitterness, and anger, even if it means sacrificing our own money, time, abilities, or pride to set someone else free.

The Spirit of God unleashed a flood of anointing at New Birth early in January 1998 when He spoke to my heart about making a personal Jubilee sacrifice and a public announcement. I was praying the Lord's Prayer and minding my own business, but when I reached the part of the prayer that says, "Forgive us our debts," the Lord stopped me.

I went back over the prayer again from the beginning, and when I got to that same place, the Lord stopped me again. I said, "Forgive us our debts, as we forgive our debtors. Lead us not . . . " and He said, "No, stop right there. You have already prayed that you would not enter into temptation, and I have already given you your daily bread. Your problem is *forgiving your debtors*." That is when God told me, "Today, you are to cancel every debt that is owed to you."

Now that may not have much of an impact on you as you read these words, but I helped put two people into business. It took a lot more than just a few thousand dollars to help launch those two businesses, and I did it out of my own pocket because I didn't want to come to the church. Then there was another situation in which I had pooled together enough of my own money to help save another church from bankruptcy.

After the Lord spoke to me, I called up the pastor of that church that very same day; he knew my phone call was personal. In fact, he thought I was calling to ask him where the money was that he owed me, so he started to talk. I interrupted him and said, "You don't need to say anything. God told me this morning to tell you that your debt is canceled. Go and do what God has ordained to be done."

When that pastor realized that I was canceling his debt, he was overwhelmed and in tears. Both of us knew it was God. (At the time, I didn't have a release from the Lord to tell the people how much debt He had asked me to forgive and release, but later on I was permitted to tell them that the amount owed me for helping with the two businesses and the church totaled eighty-six thousand dollars.)

God said to us, "To the extent that you are able to forgive debt, I will forgive yours. I cannot release the spirit of Jubilee over you until you do something. You have to do something. You have to confess it and claim it, or you can't walk in it."

So I told the congregation, "There are people in the sanctuary right now who may owe you money. When I spoke to you about what God did in me, you already sensed in your spirit that you are supposed to cancel their debts. I want you to stand and come to this altar." As the altars were flooded with people responding to God's word, I told them:

> You are to call the people who owe you money and tell them, "In Jesus' name, your debt is canceled." There must be a release in the spirit realm so that God can equip you and bless you for the Year of Jubilee. Jesus told us to pray, "Forgive us our debts, *as we forgive our debtors.*" Do not say this with remorse. Do it with joy. If your debtor still wants to bless you by paying you back or at least contributing a partial payment, fine—but that is not your objective.
>
> Tell your debtor, "In Jesus' name, your debt is canceled. Now go and do what the Lord said." God does not want you to be sad. You are going to see some things happening in your finances because of your act of obedience.
>
> Lift your hands and repeat after me: "Father, right now, in this Year of Jubilee, because I have crossed over the storms of adversity and because You have been so faithful, I will be faithful. I am canceling the debts owed to me right now, in the name of Jesus. Lord, release the spirit of Jubilee upon me and my bloodline, right now, in the name of Jesus. Lord, I thank You, and I receive it in Jesus' name."

At that point I felt impressed by the Lord to do something that may have been unique to that time and place; I don't know. You will have to gauge that for yourself. I told everyone—including those who had publicly forgiven debts owed to them—that God wanted them to do something else by faith as an act of obedience for the Year of Jubilee. I told them to make out a check or give an offering to the church (not to me) for $19.98 as a token of obedience. Then they were to list their debts on a special form that would be placed on the altar the following weekend.

That debt list wasn't for the benefit of man; it was a written petition to be presented to God because He said prophetically, "Watch Me start to cancel debt." I told the congregation that they were releasing a manifestation of God's favor that was going to start moving so quickly in their lives that it would be astounding. And it happened just as I knew it would.

As the congregation responded with supernatural joy, the spirit of Jubilee was released in that place! People who didn't have cars found people coming up to them with keys in their hands, saying things like, "Here are the keys. It's the white Honda in the back parking lot. It's yours." Other folks volunteered to pay off mortgages, credit card debts, and hospital bills. The whole house was swept up with a liberal spirit of giving and the supernatural faith to reach out and help others. I have never seen anything like it.

God said, "To the extent that you are able to forgive debt, I will forgive yours. I cannot release the spirit of Jubilee over you until you do something." I can honestly say that I have not missed any of the eighty-six thousand dollars from which I released my debtors. Better yet, God did such a work in the local church that we weren't content just to talk about what God did that day in January. The Holy Spirit moved upon our congregation to make a very unusual commitment—especially in light of the fact that we are in the middle of building a forty-million dollar facility to handle our skyrocketing growth over the last three years! The congregation made a commitment to ensure that every single female head of household in the fellowship had transportation. Many have been set free because the body of Christ moved as God ordained in the freeing of others.

In a nutshell, the deepest meaning of the Year of Jubilee is found in restoring all that which in the course of time was perverted by man's sin. God is saying that in our "practice and training" for the race of the kingdom—in our mistakes and mess-ups, in our foolishness in running all of our credit cards to the maximum limits of our credit, in the divorces we came through, in the bankruptcies, in all of our ignorance and sin—we did not know Him. There was a time when we worshiped "the unknown God" and all of life's calamities were heaped upon us. Then when it was time to run the race, we were still bound by past mistakes, failures, shortcomings, and entanglements. We desperately needed someone to instantly cancel that unpayable debt, to snap that unbreakable bondage so we could be free to run. Jesus our Jubilee has done that. He has supplied everything we need to be free and to free others in His name.

Let me return to Leviticus 25:9, which says, "Then you shall cause the trumpet of the Jubilee to sound on the tenth day of the seventh month; on the Day of Atonement you shall make the trumpet to sound throughout all your land." I need to emphasize once again that we cannot celebrate Jubilee if we have not made a conscious effort to forgive our enemies. We cannot sit in the congregation of the Lord and have a bad attitude toward someone else. We have no business carrying grudges, angry memories, unforgiveness, and bitterness from years gone by, and then putting on a party hat and expecting God to bless our mess! He is telling the church to raise its standards to match His holiness. Nothing happens in the kingdom until we observe and honor atonement, until we forgive and are forgiven under the unifying blood of the Lamb of God.

That also means we need to stop putting one another into stereotyped boxes with religious limitations. I confess to you—with great joy and thankfulness—that I am not a purebred Baptist preacher. I'm a kind of cross-spiritualized man. I received the gift of the Holy Spirit and began to speak in tongues at a Jimmy Swaggart convention. (Yes, I said a Jimmy Swaggart convention.)

Oddly enough, it was my ex-wife, the woman who

would tell you she hated church and anything connected with the ministry, who made me go to that meeting. I didn't want to go hear Jimmy Swaggart. I didn't like Jimmy, even though that was back in Jimmy's popular days before his personal problems made the headlines and the evening news. So I went to Jimmy Swaggart's meeting and got filled with the Holy Ghost.

I knew I was anointed by God for great leadership the day I was watching Dr. Charles Stanley minister on television the Sunday morning before I preached my first sermon at the first church I pastored. Now Dr. Stanley is generally known as noncharismatic, but it sure seemed to please God to use Dr. Stanley's ministry to touch me with the same anointing I carry to this day!

Never underestimate the power of God in a humble and obedient servant—no matter what man-made title has been attached to him. All I know is that I got down on my knees when Dr. Stanley asked his congregation and the people watching by television to pray. All of a sudden I felt a warm oil from the very presence of God flow over me; it totally broke me. I cried uncontrollably all the way to church. That's not a bad result for a supposedly noncharismatic TV preacher, is it?

God has a way of blunting criticism before it even gets out of people's lips. Even as I write these words, I can almost hear some of the comments: "What is Bishop Long talking about? Why, he's a Black bishop in a Black denomination. He's writing a Black book for Black people—now what does Jimmy Swaggart have to do with it anyway? And how did Dr. Stanley, a White Southern Baptist preacher who doesn't even believe in speaking in tongues, get in the picture?"

No, we are talking about a product of God. When God preordains a thing, it pleases Him to move heaven and earth—and even a boatload of crusty, hard-hearted, change-hating Christians—to see His purpose come to pass. In my case it pleased almighty God to use a teary-eyed, hard-preaching, White, Assemblies of God, pentecostal preacher who later fell into immorality to get me thoroughly baptized in the Holy Ghost. Then He moved me into position in front of a TV set on the very morning I launched my pastoral ministry to watch a calm, dignified, and highly educated Southern Baptist preacher so He could anoint me for church-changing leadership. God didn't ask my opinion on the matter, and I know He sure didn't ask yours!

We all need to stop being judgmental. It is time to lay down our preconceived prejudices based on skin color, economic status, denominational background, education, and personal preferences. We need to acknowledge our debts to one another and rejoice in God's ability to bring unity in the midst of diversity. This heart of agreement and acceptance is inseparable from the Year of Jubilee because it is the way of Christ.

There is another side to the Year of Jubilee that most people want to skip over (to their own loss). Listen to what the Lord says:

> That fiftieth year shall be a Jubilee to you; in it you shall neither sow nor reap what grows of its own accord, nor gather the grapes of your untended vine. For it is the Jubilee; it shall be holy to you; you shall eat its produce from the field.
>
> —LEVITICUS 25:11–12

Did you notice God's command not to sow, reap, or gather in Jubilee? Why is God saying this? God anticipated our every question and fear, explaining:

> And if you say, "What shall we eat in the seventh year, since we shall not sow nor gather in our produce?" Then I will command My blessing on you in the sixth year, and it will bring forth produce enough for three years. And you shall sow in the

eighth year, and eat old produce until the ninth year; until its produce comes in, you shall eat of the old harvest.

—LEVITICUS 25:20–22

God is saying to the church today, "I have already given you enough bread. I have given you enough Word in the previous years to sustain you in total supply and victory for three more years! I have given you enough of My revelation and authority to set you free from every bondage, difficulty, and obstacle entangling you and those around you. I have given you enough of My wisdom and power to cancel every debt, heal every sickness, restore every broken home and marriage, and fully establish and equip the body of Christ for the next generation."

God has fed us very well, but we have been sitting and doing nothing with it. It is time to rest in the revelation and supply that God has already given us. It is time to reach out and bless others with God's abundant supply of blessings. That is the real purpose of Jubilee!

The people in God's congregation who need to be set free in Jubilee are in the minority—most of us rejoice in God's abundant blessings, and we live in a good measure of freedom and power already. The majority of us in the kingdom are to *take the benefits of Jubilee* to those in bondage and lack. We are to embody Jubilee to those around us.

God has *already* set us free with His Word, His Son, and His Spirit. Whatever need or difficulty you have, the word of command, release, and supply has already spoken your release in the Year of Jubilee. God says you must go back and receive it.

6

I THINK I'M PREGNANT

When God gives you a promise, more than anything else it is a promise that *things are going to change*—especially *you!* In fact, He will allow just enough time to pass before that promise is fulfilled to seriously challenge most of what you know about Him. I've noticed that it always seems to take *more* faith to make it from the latest promise to the possession of it than it did "the last time."

Sarah, the wife of Abraham, knew a lot about change. She had much in common with the church today. In fact, Sarah and the church are more alike than most of us want to admit.

> Then they said to him, "Where is Sarah your wife?" So he said, "Here, in the tent." And He [the Lord] said, "I will certainly return to you according to the time of life, and behold, Sarah your wife shall have a

son." (Sarah was listening in the tent door which was behind him.)

Now Abraham and Sarah were old, well advanced in age; and Sarah had passed the age of childbearing.

—Genesis 18:9–11

When God first speaks to you, you get so excited that you just have to tell somebody. That excitement keeps going for a day or so, or maybe even for a whole week. After all, God said it, so it is going to happen immediately, right? When it doesn't happen when you think it should happen, you get anxious. You wonder if maybe you should "help God" just a little bit to make sure His promise comes true. Then you start feeling different.

The more time goes by, the more you feel as if life has passed you by, too. You could be sixteen or eighty-six, but when God plants a promise in your heart, you have to *expect* something to happen long *before* you see that promise fulfilled. You should also expect some serious changes to come your way. You have to expand some things to make room for God's promise, and that process isn't usually attractive or exciting—it's painful. Most of the time we reach a point where we question whether we heard God or just "ate too much of a good thing" late one night and fed some overactive dreams. We are tempted to say what Satan said in the beginning: "Maybe God *really* meant..."

YOU HAVEN'T HAD THE BEST...YET

Abraham and Sarah experienced a serious delay between the day Abraham received God's promise and the day Isaac was born. I don't think we would have made it.

It is amazing that so many of us in the church are living with the firm belief that we have already had the best. God is saying, "You haven't had the best—the best is yet to come." The things that you think have passed you by have not—they are still in front of you. The church needs to understand that her most glorious days are still ahead. We cannot go back and recapture the glory of the two Great Awakening revivals, and we don't need to. The most glorious days of the church are yet to come.

Understand that God does not move backward, from more to less. No, He is moving in greater glory, as the Scripture says:

> But we all, with unveiled face, beholding as in a mirror the glory of the Lord, are being transformed into the same image from glory to glory, just as by the Spirit of the Lord.
>
> —2 CORINTHIANS 3:18

But our response to God's greatest (or most impossible) promises for our lives is usually the same as Sarah's:

> And He [the Lord] said, "I will certainly return to you according to the time of life, and behold, Sarah your wife shall have a son." (Sarah was listening in the tent door which was behind him.)
>
> Now Abraham and Sarah were old, well advanced in age; and Sarah had passed the age of child-bearing. Therefore Sarah laughed within herself, saying, "After I have grown old, shall I have pleasure, my lord being old also?"
>
> And the LORD said to Abraham, "Why did Sarah laugh, saying, 'Shall I surely bear a child, since I am old?' Is anything too hard for the LORD? At the appointed time I will return to you, according to the time of life, and Sarah shall have a son."
>
> But Sarah denied it, saying, "I did not laugh," for she was afraid. And He said, "No, but you did laugh!"
>
> —GENESIS 18:10–15

First Sarah expressed her doubt and unbelief in secret, forgetting that God hears the thoughts and intents of our heart. When the Lord confronted her, she denied it, saying, "I did not laugh." Why? The answer reveals one of the biggest problems in the church. The Bible says Sarah was *afraid*. (Once again, doesn't this sound like what happened in the Garden of Eden?)

Whether you realize it or not, all of this ties in directly to your own personal calling and destiny in God. The Lord is speaking to each of us in the church today, and we need to know what we are facing—within and without. Our biggest problem isn't the devil and his demons—they are defeated foes. Our biggest problem is much closer to home. It is the same problem Sarah faced: herself.

THE CHURCH HAS A SIGHT PROBLEM

Sarah was a woman who basically had lost her faith because of her assessment in the natural. One of the greatest problems in the church today is our "sight problem." We see everything in the natural, but we insist on calling ourselves spiritual beings. Once we conclude that God has "missed His mark" and failed to come through on a promise, we feel we should "help" Him along.

Perhaps you have been dealing with some serious problems in your marriage or on the job for about three years, yet God told you a long time ago, "I am going to fix this." Since three years have gone by with no noticeable change, you have settled in and accepted the situation. So when God says it is time to *change,* you will not accept it *because of what you see* and what you have been through over the last thirty-six months. Can you see what happened? You lowered your aim; you lived with a low expectancy. "I don't even want to get excited anymore, God."

GOD WANTS TO IMPREGNATE THE CHURCH

You may think it crude, but this expression could hardly be more theologically and spiritually accurate. God isn't prudish like us. Sex and marriage are the Lord's greatest picture of His mysterious relationship with the church. When we turn prudish, we turn away from one of God's greatest prophetic tools for discerning His will and His ways!

God is looking for a womb, but we're not expecting to *birth* anything. What do we really *expect* when we come into the presence of the Lord? Look at the body of Christ in North America and around the world. We cannot settle in and think that everything is as good as it can be— because it's not! Don't settle for less than the fullness of God's promises. Enter into His presence with joy and great expectancy.

Sarah could not believe God's promise that she would become pregnant and deliver a son—it was too difficult to believe because all the natural signs pointed to the fact that her seed-bearing days had passed. That which God promised was impossible now—it would take a miracle. It was too good to be true. Sarah's faith was paralyzed by her fear. Her sudden fear caused her to shift into "spiritual birth control" mode.

God is looking for a womb in the earth. He is looking for a people who are so built up with faith that they will "boldly go where few saints have ever gone before." He is looking for people who have grown in their faith to the point that they do not need a lot of evidence to believe God. Understand this: *As your faith grows, your need for evidence decreases*. God isn't interested in giving you a lot of signs to prove that what He said is going to come true. In fact, as your faith increases, He will pull away evidence because He is looking for someone who will move just because He says, "Move."

TAKING OVER

STOP CALLING GOD "SATAN"!

The Lord is stirring up His church, looking for a faithful womb, and we think it is the devil at work. Listen, the devil ain't bothering you. Stop calling God "Satan." It is God who is waking you up at night! It is God who is bringing changes to your life. He is causing the discomfort because He is looking for a faithful womb.

When you talk about a womb, you are talking about birth and the arrival of something new. Many in the body of Christ worldwide, and particularly in the United States, understand that we need something new; something needs to change.

ARE YOU FAITHFUL ENOUGH TO BE A FOOL?

God is looking for a womb. He is looking for someone who is faithful enough to be ridiculous and do foolish things by faith. If you don't even have a high school diploma, you can still make it in this world as long as you have Jesus. You are a prime candidate for God's plan to confound somebody who thinks he or she is wise. All you have to do is turn over your life to the Lord and say, "Lord, I don't have much education, but I'm willing to do whatever You want me to do. If You want me to go to college and blow the minds of the professors, I am willing. I want to be a living example."

God is looking for people who are willing to die to themselves to accomplish the works and will of God. I was profoundly touched while preaching to my congregation about family relationships from Ephesians 5. I had reached the controversial area of wives submitting themselves to their husbands, and I was telling husbands to love their wives as Christ loved the church and gave Himself for it. (See Ephesians 5:25–26.) I explained to the husbands that if their wives were not acting the way they should in their opinion, then the husbands had to die to themselves *first*. I said, "You were not acting the way you should have been acting *until Christ died first*. So you have to die first so your wife can be perfected."

As I studied this chapter in private, I kept reading until I reached the passage where Paul said in effect, "Well, you should know that what I'm really talking about is a great mystery. I'm really talking about Christ and the church." (See Ephesians 5:32.) Then I got real spiritual and said in my best King James accent, "What sayest this, Lord?"

God reminded me of this verse in 1 Samuel:

> Now the boy Samuel ministered to the LORD before Eli. And the word of the LORD was rare in those days; there was no widespread revelation.
>
> —1 SAMUEL 3:1

Let me explain what God was saying to me. I am linking Paul's statement about the mystery of Christ and the church to God's statement about a lack of revelation in Samuel's day because they reveal these fundamental principles:

- If there is no peace in the house, there will be no peace in the church.

- If wives will not submit themselves to their husbands in the house, they will not submit themselves to the headship of the church.

- If husbands refuse to die at home and take the responsibility God gave them, then they will not die as men in the church.

WHEN GOD DOESN'T SPEAK, NOTHING NEW IS FORMED

My point is that the living Word of God is potent. This point is so important that I am compelled to use the most powerful (and graphic) picture that God has given us in the natural realm: The Word of God is His sperm. Think about God's statement: "There was no widespread revelation." What He was saying is, "There were no widespread pregnancies taking place." If you think I'm being outrageous and out of line with my reasoning, then I urge you to read the Gospel of Luke the physician:

> "And behold, you will conceive in your womb and bring forth a Son, and shall call His name JESUS...."
>
> Then Mary said to the angel, "How can this be, since I do not know a man?" And the angel answered and said to her, "The Holy Spirit will come upon you, and the power of the Highest will overshadow you; therefore, also, that Holy One who is to be born will be called the Son of God...."
>
> Then Mary said, "Behold the maidservant of the Lord! Let it be to me according to your word." And the angel departed from her.
>
> —LUKE 1:31, 34–35, 38

The world was formed when God *spoke*. When God doesn't speak, nothing is created; nothing new enters the world. If God's living Word is the supernatural "sperm" of God's anointing coming from the ministry gift standing before His people, then guess what the local church is? The church is the womb of God. Every living word from the heart of God that is spoken is supposed to be taken in by the womb.

In the natural realm, the womb doesn't "fall" on the sperm; the womb takes in the sperm. The womb doesn't think about whether it's going to receive it; the womb just makes it happen. The womb incubates the received seed of God and carries it to full term until it is delivered into the earth. The womb carries and labors over God's seed.

Our problem is that most of the preachers in America's

churches today are disseminating "dead sperm." A lot of preachers are preaching warmed-over, store-bought, convention sermons prepared by other men in other places. Yes, they may be giving their congregations a word, but it is not a "word in season." They are not providing a fresh revelation of God to their people. We can read and memorize God's Word all we want, but if we don't spend time in the presence of God, laboring before Him and ministering to Him, then nothing is going to be *fresh*. Paul wrote, "[God] made us sufficient as ministers of the new covenant, not of the letter but of the Spirit; *for the letter kills, but the Spirit gives life*" (2 Cor. 3:6, italics added).

Such preaching is powerless to impregnate God's people with His anointed vision. Preachers are dying before their time because they are trying to make the sperm serve as the womb as well. The job of the preacher is to labor before God in His presence to "bring fresh sperm." The job of the church, the womb of God, is to receive God's seed and say, "Yes, Lord, let it be to me according to Your Word. We are going to make this happen!"

TURN ON THE LOVE MUSIC AND CONCEIVE SOMETHING NEW

I'm already out on a limb, so I'll just take this a little further. Do you know why we praise the Lord before the Word comes forth? We praise God to create glory. We are turning on the "love music," if you will. We are setting the atmosphere and clouding up the room with smoky incense of prayers, praise, and adoration. (I know you may be feeling uncomfortable at this point, but you will get over it if you get the point.) The romancing begins when we say from the heart, "I love You, Lord. I'm getting ready to conceive something holy and birth something for You in the earth."

I'm so far out on this limb right now that I might as well cut it all the way off and say this: The problem with most churches is that *they want a lot of foreplay with no conception in the Holy Ghost.*

We come into God's presence bearing our "spiritual contraceptives"! We don't want to conceive anything that God has for us because *we don't want to change.* We don't want to hear it. We don't want to make it happen. All we want is to just come together and have a good time. We don't want to bother with all of the hassles of commitment and sacrifice. And above all, we want to avoid *pregnancy.*

Does that sound familiar? It ought to! The self-centered things going on in the back seats of cars *started in the church.* "You mean You want sacrifice? No! You mean You want me to give an offering? No! You mean You want us to buy a building? No! You mean You want me to leave my comfortable home to go into that neighborhood with You? No!"

As a Black preacher, I'm going to say something straight to the Black segments of the church: Do you know why Black churches major in storefront buildings? I believe it is because many of the congregations just won't make it happen. They have rejected the Word of God, the sperm of God—because in the natural realm it is impossible. That's why predominately Black congregations don't have television and radio stations or major recording studios.

I asked the Lord, "Why does it look as though the devil has more power than You?" He answered, "There has *never* been a time when the devil has had more power than I have. Satan has been operating according to modern spiritual warfare methods while the church is still stuck in 1960."

YOU REAP BARRENNESS WHEN YOU REJECT GOD'S SEED

Whatever the devil speaks, his army brings to pass. But

when the men and women of God speak, the church rejects their words and aborts the vision of God. The only change we've had since the 1960s is that we have finally added praise—or more "foreplay." You may not want to shout about this point, but it is the truth. God is once again surveying the earth and saying, "There is no widespread revelation—My Word is rare in these days."

The church, the womb of God, rejects the seed of God and then complains and wonders why God isn't revealing His glory in the earth today! We reap what we sow, or in the case of God's womb, we reap a harvest of barrenness when we abort or reject the seed of God. The naysaying church should look at Mary and ask, "What if Mary had said, 'There's no way I am going to be used by God to birth such a thing in the earth. It's embarrassing, it's dangerous, and it's an invasion of my privacy. I have my own life to live. Check with somebody else.'"

Let me ask this: If we have been hearing the inspired Word of God preached for the last ten years, then why are we doing the same things we've been doing for the last ten years? Consider the young boy Samuel. The voice of God came to him three times before he realized what was going on. Each time Samuel checked with old Eli and was told, "I didn't call you. Go back to bed."

Isn't it funny that when we *really* hear the voice of God, we often take that precious seed to somebody else—a friend, a prayer partner, or a preacher—for verification? We check with the existing system to see if it's God.

"I hear God telling me to do something real silly. Do you think this is right?"

"Well, child, *ain't nobody else ever done that.* I don't think you should. If it was that necessary, somebody else would have done it."

"You're right."

Why would we need *faith* to do something somebody else has done already? God is not looking for a repeat performance from us. He moves from glory to glory, from one level to the next level, from faith to greater faith. How many times have we allowed people—even church folk—and the extra-biblical rules and regulations of church systems to *talk us out of the revelation of God?* How can flesh and blood tell us what God is about to do?

Our problem in the church is that we think everything God does has to conform to our existing system and structure—even though we already agree it doesn't work! Why do we keep doing what doesn't work? When God answers our prayers and says, "Do this," we don't; we explain to God and everyone else, "Well, nobody else has ever done it before." But we are more than ready to continue doing things that don't work (after all, *everybody* has done that before). Listen—even my little boy has the sense to say, "Daddy, that hasn't been working. Try something different."

After Samuel woke up Eli for the third time, the old priest finally realized God *might* be doing something He hadn't done for a long while. So Eli said, "If you hear that voice again, you sit up in your bed and say, 'Speak, Lord, for Your servant hears.'" (See 1 Samuel 3:9.)

ARE YOU HEARING GOD'S FOURTH CALL?

I am thoroughly convinced that God is speaking to everyone who will listen to His creative Word. Count on it: God is not going to do something that He did before. He is looking for someone who has enough faith to declare, "If nobody else is going to go with God on this thing, then I am just going to sit up and say, 'Speak, Lord, for Your servant hears.'"

Do you want to know whether or not you are hearing God's fourth call? When you thought you heard God speak to you, did you tell your friends about it, yet they just couldn't understand what you were saying? You used to be able to talk to them and come into agreement, but now they can't even understand what you're saying. Do you find yourself thinking, *I've got to keep this stuff to myself. Now that I'm hearing a voice, the devil is trying to say I'm crazy.*

You aren't crazy. God is creating something new. God is speaking fresh things into your heart and life. All those nights you thought something was wrong with you, God was waking you up to talk to you (not to haunt you). If this is the fourth time, then you need to *listen* to Him and obey.

God is keeping you up at night and calling you close because you told Him you are tired of the same old pattern of playing church. You are tired of jumping in church services when everybody else is jumping (even though you don't feel a thing or don't sense God within a mile of the place). You are tired of everything that points to the failure of the church to *be* the church to a lost world.

God is saying, "I'm tired of it, too! I am looking for a people who are ready to hear Me and obey. When I speak, you will change. You won't be able to play that instrument as you used to play it." The only comment you used to get was, "Oooh, there's an anointing on that organ." No, the anointing doesn't come from the organ! Once God speaks and you hear Him, you will discover a *new sound* coming from your life. If you are a musician, don't be afraid to break from what everybody else has been writing and playing—you know it hasn't been changing anybody's life anyway! You are pregnant. God's hand is upon you to birth something *new* in the earth.

Now I want you to pay close attention to what God told Samuel once He had his full attention the fourth time around:

> Then the LORD said to Samuel: "Behold, I will do something in Israel at which both ears of everyone who hears it will tingle. In that day I will perform against Eli all that I have spoken concerning his house, from beginning to end. For I have told him that I will judge his house forever for the iniquity

which he knows, because his sons made themselves vile, and he did not restrain them."

—1 SAMUEL 3:11–13

God told Samuel, "I'm getting ready to get rid of the old system." Whoever heard of Mark Hanby, Donald Wright, or T. D. Jakes eight years ago? The only people we knew about then were the "kings of the gospel" who were running around building their private empires and keeping private intrigues behind closed doors. I am referring specifically to those individuals and religious associations that have publicly built things outside of God's biblical order. They honored their own agendas, names, and accomplishments above those of God Himself.

However, the many faithful ministers of God who are important and anointed exceptions to this rule will *not* be moved out; they will be promoted as God's generals and grandfathers of the faith to raise up and train younger leaders in God's way.

God is telling us today, "The old system I never ordained or blessed, that old prostitute system is out, and I am raising up new folks of whom you have never heard."

GOD REMOVES THE OLD BEFORE
HE BEGINS THE NEW

The Lord always takes away the first so He can bring in the latter. When God starts to work on your life, He will begin to move out the things you had made anchors in your life. If you always depend on Sister So-and-So to come through when you were down, you will discover her line is suddenly busy all the time. Now you will have to get on your knees and seek Him instead. She was a blessing for a season, but she isn't God.

God will change your mind by cleaning out your old ways of thinking. You thought that it was the devil who robbed you of your financial security when you were suddenly laid off. You thought your friend, Sister So-and-So, deliberately betrayed you and wouldn't return your calls. No, God made it inconvenient for that company to keep you. He made it impossible for the good sister to call you. You thought it was the devil, but it was God just taking away your old way of thinking and living. He is moving you into position for a miracle, and the only position worthy of a miracle is a position of desperate faith.

Sarah was ninety years old when God promised her a son, and the thought of getting pregnant was probably frightening to her. If God has been talking to you, then I have news for you. You and Sarah share something in common. You had better watch for some unusual changes in your life. When my wife became pregnant, we didn't know it at first. A few weeks later, Vanessa told me she was "feeling funny." I said, "Honey, you need to go to the drug store and get one of those home pregnancy test kits. We need to see what is going on."

Sure enough, our do-it-yourself pregnancy test was positive (and the doctor later confirmed it "officially"). Vanessa didn't get any better; she started feeling funny all of the time. She just wasn't feeling like herself. Then she started stretching. When you attend an anointed Bible or church conference, you may find yourself feeling funny; then you discover that you are being stretched. You didn't know it, but you opened up your spirit just long enough to get pregnant with a holy seed from God. There is *change* in your future.

You need to understand this important kingdom principle: *Revelation never comes in its mature state.* When you first get pregnant with a vision or message from God, you receive the seed of the revelation. It has to get *in you* before it can grow and begin to stretch you. I can guarantee you this much: That holy thing is going to work in you. If you received the principle I just gave you, then *you just got pregnant.* Now you will have to go through the process of nurturing what you've received from God's

Spirit. It follows a pattern of unstoppable growth as you carry it. I have to tell you that as God's seed continues to grow in you, *it might make you walk funny*.

"I LABOR IN BIRTH AGAIN UNTIL CHRIST IS FORMED"

Paul the Apostle wrote as a spiritual daddy to the spiritual children he had birthed into the kingdom of God through the preaching of the gospel: "My little children, for whom I labor in birth again until Christ is formed in you" (Gal. 4:19). Did you notice that Paul said, "My little children, for whom I labor in birth again"? That means he labored two times. Paul was saying, "My little children, whom I am calling to grow up until Christ is formed in you."

God is telling the church, "I have provided all of the living seed (sperm) you need over the last month, the last six months, the last decade, the last millennium, to make you pregnant. Your conception will immediately follow your acceptance of My Word, and in it you will find what you need to be delivered from bondage and into victory,]doing in your new birth is forming My Christ, My Anointed One, in you."

If you have been feeling stretched beyond measure, *you are pregnant*. If you haven't been feeling like yourself lately, if you have been dragging around and feeling sluggish in your spirit, it is because God impregnated you. He is forming His Son in you. No matter what form this supernatural work takes when it comes to full term, one thing is sure: With its delivery and birth, Christ will be formed even more fully in you.

What do doctors tell pregnant women? *Rest*. Once the womb has received a seed of life, a transformation begins to take place. Priorities are changed, chemical balances undergo dramatic alterations, and the entire body begins to prepare to give birth. Everything in a mother's body begins to focus on the challenging task of carrying and delivering a new life into the world. Since a pregnant woman's body is working to nourish her baby twenty-four hours a day, she needs to *rest*.

God has given you life-bearing seed, and you have received it in your heart to carry to full term and delivery. Now that you have received the word of the Lord, you are pregnant. What is being formed in you is the Son of the living God, and people will look at you and no longer see a man or a woman. They will behold the living God.

God is looking for folks who have been born again in labor. He is saying that by the time you finish this book, you are supposed to be changed. You are to go from working to resting *in what He has already done.*

7

DON'T ABORT THE PROCESS
OF MATURITY

I'm tired of seeing people hurt. I'm tired of seeing folk die before their time. I'm tired of seeing Christians shout to one another in the church, "I've got the power, the resurrection power," while they still hide themselves away in a safe building because they are afraid of drug dealers and gang-bangers half their age. I'm tired of hearing news reports about spiraling crime rates, about children being murdered in our streets and schools, and about wives and children being beaten senseless by the very men who swore to protect them. Something has to change, and we all know it.

Meanwhile, the body of Christ is scrambling aimlessly like a rat trapped in a maze, wasting its energy and losing hope as it scampers down endless paths that lead no-where. We are constantly trying to bring about something through our own efforts and religious agendas, but once we get there, we find we have little or nothing to show for all the time and energy we invested. The amazing thing about the situation is that we haven't changed our ways. We continue to blindly follow the worn path so many have followed before us until the day we die.

Do you realize that most of the things being done in the body of Christ right now were also done by your grandmother? We haven't built on the progress and maturity of our forefathers; in some cases we haven't even been able to preserve the anointing they had! You won't hear anybody say it in the church, but somebody needs to say what all of us are thinking: *We ought to change this! It isn't working. The church isn't doing anything to change the world.* But no, we're content just to keep going through the motions.

Someone who knows something ought to say something. We are in a rut, and we are doing things religiously because that's the way it has always been done. What if it has always been done that way because no one knew any better? The church has failed the primary test of God's Word: *There is no fruit being produced.* How do we know? Because nothing is really changing in our families and communities.

"Now, Bishop, it isn't all *that* bad, is it?" Let me ask you one question: How many times have you been delivered from the same thing? Here is a deep truth for you to remember: *Change is not change until it's changed.* God has a certain way of doing things, and if we reject His way in favor of our own way of doing things, we will reap the fruit of our own labors—fruitlessness.

I admit that we have to pay a high price for the lasting benefits of God's process of growth and maturity, but we pay an even higher price when we do not change! You may be sitting there right now with this book in your hands, just floating in misery because you refuse to change. It is easy to understand that you and I want to avoid change because of its high price, but we are *paying more not to change.* This is what has happened to the church.

The church around the world, and in America especially, is paying a very dear price today because we have looked at the challenge of change and said, "Oh, that is too expensive. I think I'll try an easier, quicker route." Because we refused God's challenge to change over the last few decades, we have lost our children and our families, we have given up our neighborhoods and lost our money, and many of us are even losing our minds and health. Yet few, if any, dare to say anything!

THE CHURCH IS STUCK IN A RUT OF HER OWN MAKING

Plato said, "The life which is unexamined is not worth living." Have you noticed that the church—meaning both her individual members and her public spokesmen—is very skilled and quick to criticize, protest against, and run down everybody? Then maybe you have also noticed that the church doesn't like looking at herself.

People may get angry with me, but I refuse to let this point die. I am compelled by the Spirit of God to say it is a great disgrace and a serious indictment against the church when we point our fingers of religious self-righteousness at the sin we see in the world when our own countless sins of hypocrisy and disobedience to God are heaped high within our own doors. The church is stuck in a rut of her own making; we are trapped in a maze of man-made ordinances, regulations, and authority structures that God never authored or authorized.

The church we have today is not the glorious church of power, light, and holiness pictured in the Bible. Something has to change, and God says it is about to change *now*. Judgment and mercy begin in the house of God, and then they move outward to the unredeemed world. God is determined to take away the old; then He will bring in the new.

God called us to light His lamp and stand on a hill for the

world to see, but we have insisted on having *private club meetings* instead so we can celebrate our exclusive membership in God's club without interruption from "outsiders."

We cannot ignore the fact that we almost never see an obvious change in our nation when hundreds of thousands of Christians march in Washington, D.C., or gather for other large conventions around the nation. God created *everyone* as a spiritual being, and people around this nation are desperately looking for a spiritual experience. They want to see some sign that God really exists and that He has the power to change lives for the better. The world wants to see more than an outward demonstration and show of force. The world wants to see the demonstration of a life changed within by the awesome power of God. If the church continues to fail to offer them the real thing, the people will quickly go after a counterfeit. We have to stop this mockery of God's purpose for the church.

The writer of the Book of Lamentations, the crying book, tells us:

> Let us search out and examine our ways,
> And turn back to the LORD.
> —LAMENTATIONS 3:40

WE TRY TO THWART THE MATURITY PROCESS OF GOD

While God is working to mature the people in His church by allowing them to walk through various trials, His less-discerning ministers and pastors try to preach the people out of those trials! The problem is that when people listen to that kind of preaching and start begging God for a quick fix to their long-term problem, they just might get what they are asking for. When the children of Israel were in the wilderness, they started complaining about the manna God had given them. They decided that what they needed was meat instead. So God said, "Okay, you want quail? Quail it is."

Then you [Moses] shall say to the people, "Consecrate yourselves for tomorrow, and you shall eat meat; for you have wept in the hearing of the LORD, saying, 'Who will give us meat to eat? For it was well with us in Egypt.' Therefore the LORD will give you meat, and you shall eat.

You shall eat, not one day, nor two days, nor five days, nor ten days, nor twenty days, but for a whole month, until it comes out of your nostrils and becomes loathsome to you, because you have despised the LORD who is among you, and have wept before Him, saying, 'Why did we ever come up out of Egypt?'"

—NUMBERS 11:18–20

God answered the Israelites' prayer for a quick fix, for an early deliverance from God's maturity process, but it cost them dearly. When they complained about the difficulty of their trial and longed for the good old days of slavery under Pharaoh when they had meat to eat, God gave them quail—and He also sent *leanness* to their souls. (See Psalm 106:13–15.) He was saying, "You got out too quickly. This was all part of your training. I know when it's time to bring you out of this, and I know what I'm doing. Since you feel you know better, you can reap what you have sown."

I tell the people at New Birth: "If you're going through something difficult, if you feel that you are going through hell, I have one piece of advice for you: *Don't stop.* Ask God, 'What is it You are trying to teach me? What is it You want to show me through this?'"

The church is not here to bail everybody out of their problems. I am firmly convinced that some of us in the body of Christ are *supposed* to get our houses repossessed! This may sound radical and even heretical to you, but I have to tell you that everywhere I see great victory, faith, and accomplishments in God's Word, I also see great perseverance in the face of great suffering. It is my conviction that when we preach against the process of maturity in the Christian life, we preach against *the order of God*.

God is looking for those disciples who understand that it is impossible to please God without faith. He is trying to help us grow up by marching us into such levels of maturity that we will be able to accomplish His purposes on this earth. It can only be done with the "God-kind-of-faith."

Don't write that off as a cute religious phrase. It takes God to believe God fully. (See Galatians 2:20.) When God *really* speaks to you, I can guarantee that you don't and won't have enough faith on your own to believe Him. You have to have enough God *in you* to hook up with God *speaking to you*. The only way you can accomplish the things God is calling you to do is to have so much God in you that you can believe Him supernaturally.

"Now I hope you didn't just make that up, Bishop." No, if you have a problem with this theology, then you need to talk to the Lord about it. My Bible tells me that "it is God who works in you both to will and to do for His good pleasure" (Phil. 2:13). The only thing we bring to the table of God is our obedience—even our faith must come from Him. (See Romans 12:3.) Our first and most important "work" in this life is to *believe Jesus*. Then He gives us everything we need to do the rest of the work He has called us to do.

> Jesus answered and said to them, "This is the work of God, that you believe in Him whom He sent."
>
> Therefore they said to Him, "What sign will You perform then, that we may see it and believe You? What work will You do?"
>
> —JOHN 6:29–30

WE ACT JUST LIKE THE PHARISEES WE CRITICIZE

Whenever God speaks to His Son, the Son moves immediately without conferring with flesh and blood. Now—watch this—the reason most saints and soldiers never get to the place God ordained for them is that they want to look for evidence before they move or act. We ridicule the scribes and Pharisees of Jesus' day, but then we turn around and act just like them. The moment Jesus tells us the work He's called us to do, we ask for a sign.

The second thing we do is react in fear instead of faith. That is a sure sign we haven't died to self so we can live in Christ. We are too afraid of losing our self to live for Him. This robs us of the faith of God residing within us. We say, "God, that's *impossible*. I can't do that. It's too big for me. I'm afraid. I might get killed. I can't go there. I can't do that."

I'm convinced our problem isn't that we haven't heard God. We've heard His voice all right; we are just too afraid to do what God has ordained. We are too busy looking for a sign as all of the crowds that followed Jesus did; then they backed off when the risk of obedience became too great.

> But the boat was now in the middle of the sea, tossed by the waves, for the wind was contrary. Now in the fourth watch of the night Jesus went to them, walking on the sea. And when the disciples saw Him walking on the sea, they were troubled, saying, "It is a ghost!" And they cried out for fear.
>
> But immediately Jesus spoke to them, saying, "Be of good cheer! It is I; do not be afraid."
>
> And Peter answered Him and said, "Lord, if it is You, command me to come to You on the water."
>
> So He said, "Come." And when Peter had come down out of the boat, he walked on the water to go to Jesus. But when he saw that the wind was boisterous, he was afraid; and beginning to sink he cried out, saying, "Lord, save me!"
>
> And immediately Jesus stretched out His hand and caught him, and said to him, "O you of little faith, why did you doubt?" And when they got into the boat, the wind ceased.

> Then those who were in the boat came and wor-
> shiped Him, saying, "Truly You are the Son of God."
> —MATTHEW 14:24–33

Our situation is serious. Change has to happen in the church today. God is looking for some crazy Peters who will dare to take risks at His command, even in the middle of a storm. I don't know about you, but I can't remember when I *wasn't* living in a storm. There has always been a storm of some kind blowing and tossing things around in my life. That doesn't mean God wasn't there or that I am some kind of faithless Christian. My biggest problem was that most of the time, *I was acting like the eleven* instead of like crazy Peter, the one who dared to step out of the boat of his security when Jesus said, "Come."

I am like you. I always had what I thought were good reasons and excuses to stay in the boat. But God is looking for someone who will stop complaining about the storm long enough to hear and obey His voice. If He says, "Walk on the water," He doesn't want us to ask questions; He wants us to just start walking.

Now you may be saying, "Bishop, my Bible says Peter started to sink." Yes, my Bible says the same thing. Why? Peter began to sink because he took his eyes off Jesus the Rock and instead looked at the circumstances—the wind and the waves.

COWERING IN THE "BOAT OF WHAT WAS"

I am convinced that Peter, the professional sailor and fisherman, had already seen those waves; he had mea-sured the intensity of the wind long before he stepped out of the boat. He had already assessed those problems, yet he dismissed them when he heard his Master's voice.

But something helped him turn his eyes away from Jesus and onto those old circumstances again, and I think his problem was that the wind was talking. You see, whenever the wind blows, it can carry voices with it. There were eleven frightened (and probably jealous) men who were still cowering in the boat of man's ingenuity, telling Peter to get back on the "firm" wooden deck of the "boat of what was."

"You can't do that, Peter. How can you *know* that is really Jesus? After all, that is a *spirit* out there. You are messing us up. We need your strong back at the oars. Get back on this boat!" I think there is a good chance that Peter started listening to the crowd for just a moment— and the crowd has never been right as far as God's kingdom goes. God has never led, fed, or said something by majority vote. No, God is *still* looking for somebody who will step away from everybody else and dare to obey His challenge to change.

The problem with most church folk is that they need a crowd to think they are following God. It is true that crowds gathered where Jesus went, but only disciples followed Christ to the cross and beyond. That's the reason why our churches are only half full for intercessory prayer meetings and work days. The other half is following the crowd. That is why only a handful will show up for the evangelism outreach trip to the wrong side of the tracks; the rest of the "gang of eleven" are clinging to the "home boat" and griping about the few who said *yes* to change.

IF GOD SAID IT, IT WILL TAKE GOD TO PULL IT OFF

We just don't want to go through God's process. We would rather stay in the old system and cling to the old stuff that doesn't work. We don't want to be enlarged because it stretches us beyond our comfort zone. I can promise you this: Whatever God wants you to do right now as an individual and as a member of a local body of believers cannot be accomplished with the narrow and shallow foundation you have today. He has to enlarge and stretch you.

When God places a call or vision in your life, by definition it is *supernatural*. It cannot ever be accomplished with your strength, resources, or abilities. It will take God to pull it off, so why even play the game of saying, "God, I can't do it"? Of course you can't! Why would God ask you to do something that you could do in your own strength? You wouldn't need His provision, His wisdom, or His power to do it. In other words, it would then be a work of the flesh. Trust me, God doesn't work that way.

God wants to pull you out of your boat today because He's about to lay something on the church that is going to revolutionize the world! He is saying, "I need steadfast, immovable, always abounding people. I need people who have been through the fire, people who came through with My Word clenched in their fists. I'm looking for the kind of people who know what it means to break through impossible situations with My Word. They have been *stretched* with My Word and still managed to hang on, even when it seemed that the thing I promised them wasn't going to happen. I'm looking for a people who consented to go all the way through the process and emerged with enlarged spirits, vision, and faith."

God is looking for people who have mountain-moving faith! Jesus said, "Assuredly, I say to you, if you have faith as a mustard seed, you will say to this mountain, 'Move from here to there,' and it will move; and nothing will be impossible for you" (Matt. 17:20).

I live right near the base of Stone Mountain near Atlanta, Georgia. I confess that there were times when I used to feel extra "spiritual," and I would go up to Stone Mountain and say, "Mountain, move." Now even though I "did what the Bible said," that mountain didn't move.

Then I got some sense after the Holy Ghost said, "Son, don't speak to *that* mountain. Speak to whatever mountain mounts up in your presence in opposition to My revealed will for your life and those in your care. Then you can command it to get out of the way, but not by *your* might or power. Speak the word of command by the Spirit."

THINGS SEEM TO GET WORSE BEFORE THEY GET BETTER

I looked a little closer at the mustard seed in Jesus' statements. The mustard seed is so small that it is hard to conceive of it being worthy of mention in a teaching on mountain-moving power. When you realize that Jesus mentioned the mustard seed in the context of something that you plant in the ground, things get even stranger. This little seed is so small that it can barely be seen above ground; then it must be buried in the ground out of sight before it can produce anything. You have to put a little dirt on it and compress soil on top of it—in other words, it goes through the process of death and burial.

In a way, this is the same process you and I go through every time we get pregnant with God's promise. Things just seem to get worse before they get better—but nothing is wrong. It is just the process of God.

Now when that tiny mustard seed is separated from the other mustard seeds and removed from the light of day, from the wind, and from the life-sustaining rain, its only company is darkness and dirt. I thank God that He designed seeds not to operate by sight. In a sense, the darkness and dirt are telling the seed, "You aren't getting out—you are just a tiny seed caught in our grip far from the light. You are dead."

Even as you read these words, you may feel as if you have already been eulogized by the darkness, and the dirt has been piled on top of you. You have heard it all: "This is your lot in life. You are stuck in this place! You'll never taste joy again. You will never have pleasure in your life. You are old. You are sick and weak. You're condemned to die where you lie."

Take courage from the tiny mustard seed that says:

I am not a seed. I may look like a seed, but I'm really a giant tree. In God's perfect time I am going to be a tree. After a while I'm coming up out of this darkness and exploding from the dirt into the light. Then I will be the master over the dirt, and I will draw strength from the very thing that tried to bury me. So you can talk about me today, you can pick on me for a season, but I believe what God says about me. No matter what you say or do, I'm going to keep saying, "I'm a tree. I'm a tree. I'm a tree!"

How does that old saying go? "Every mighty oak tree began as a nut that just kept going." If God says your marriage will be resurrected, then don't be surprised if that promise gets buried by mountains of dirt and darkness. Your job is to keep talking about resurrection.

If God tells you He has destroyed the yoke of poverty over your life, then keep speaking the promise of prosperity, even though you may sit in the darkness of lack under a mountain of bills for a season. See the fruit of God's favor before it appears. "I'm going to buy that, and I'm going to finance that for the kingdom. I'm going to lend money, not borrow it."

When God tells you that your church is going to take the city, then start speaking God's truth even when your enemies start lining up to "set you straight" (and they will—trust me, I've been there).

Do you know what happens millions of times a year in the Christian world of seminars, conferences, and holy convocations? Every time believers go to an anointed conference (the other kind don't count), they go home feeling wonderful, delivered, renewed, and redeemed for the first three weeks. But by the fourth or fifth week they are feeling bad again, and they find themselves sliding back into same old routine they had hoped to break by attending the conference!

JUST GREASE ME DOWN

I used to go to every conference I could find, and I went up for prayer every time I could. I should have just told those ministers, "Just grease me down with that anointing oil." I'd go to the South for a conference one week and rush to the North for another conference the next week. I did everything I could to get an instant fix to my problems without the pain of self-discipline.

I didn't want to study. I didn't want to labor. If I located an anointed man of God, I would automatically ask him lay his hands on me. I even got upset if a preacher would bypass me to lay hands on someone else. Usually I would end up chasing him down the prayer line just so I could stick my head under his hands as he prayed. It was a compulsion.

My wife tells me that once she started dilating when she was having our baby, she wondered if she was going to make it. Many women start screaming at their doctors, "Give me something! Get this kid out *now!* I quit! I don't want to do this."

Once you start having the contractions in your Holy Ghost pregnancy, you may think they are from the devil! The problem is that you will suddenly be tempted to you kick that word of promise out before its time. When you're having contractions, you need to *know* that they are from God so you can see them through to the end and possess what God has ordained for you.

EVERY SAINT OUGHT TO HAVE SOME STRETCH MARKS!

It is easy to get irritated with the growing trend among young married ladies these days who say, "Oh, I don't want to get pregnant too soon. I don't want to have any babies because I don't want to mess up my figure." This is especially hard to swallow for women who have been through some labor and deliveries. They have paid the price to give birth to new life; they have received some stretch marks in the process.

Sometimes God will stretch you when He gives you a word of promise. The holy thing you bring to term will leave some permanent marks on you, but it isn't anything to be ashamed of. Those are witnessing points.

Someone may say, "Oh, you haven't been through anything. How would you know how I feel?" Then all you have to do is open up your coat and say, "Let me show you my stretch marks. Let me tell you what will work for you. I know it will work, because it worked for me. I know what it is like to wait and wait, and then wait some more. I know what it is like to pray and fast until I thought I couldn't do it anymore—but here I am. I made it. Here are pictures of my children."

That is the same thing that Jesus did when He confronted doubting Thomas. He said, "Reach your finger here, and look at My hands; and reach your hand here, and put it into My side. Do not be unbelieving, but believing" (John 20:27).

Some of us do not want to go through the process of maturing, but it is God's divine process for birthing holy things in us, in the church, and in the world. No matter how much we want them, there are no shortcuts to God's process. He is looking for people who don't need a whole lot of evidence to move. Every time you hear God's voice and obey, your confidence is built in His Word.

Mothers who have already given birth to a child are much calmer and steadier than first-time mothers. It is the same with seasoned disciples. They aren't worried about the process of stretching, and they don't mind the discomfort and unsettled feeling of pregnancy. They know what comes at the end of God's process—new life, new joy, a new measure of power and glory, and a new horizon of opportunity in Christ.

When I first heard the call of the Lord to preach, I obeyed

because I knew I had heard His voice. I was doing well at the time—I basically took a cut in pay of thirty thousand dollars to start at my church. But later on—I said *later on*—God gave it all back to me and more.

Yet even in the place of obedience, I was in the midst of a storm because God wanted me to change. I woke up one day and said, "This thing has to be real, or I am getting out." Well, I discovered that God is *real,* and so is His power. I also discovered that there is a price attached to the real thing. Salvation is a free gift, but discipleship costs you everything. There is a cross with my name on it overshadowing my "Disciple of Jesus" badge. The badge is easy to put on, but the cross will kill you. That has been God's plan all along— kill the old man and raise up the new.

I told my congregation during a celebration of God's Year of Jubilee that the Lord was saying, "During this Year of Jubilee, your labor is going to begin. It is going to be so rough that you will have to forgive some people and get rid of all of your hidden bitterness. You see, the baby God planted in your womb is going to force every deep-rooted thing out of you."

GOD DOESN'T WANT YOU TO "FEEL LIKE YOURSELF"

You may not understand this, but during your labor to deliver God's seed in your life, He will cause the labor pains to hit you extra hard in areas where you need deliverance. Yes, you will have that baby in due time, but right now you are in the middle of this thing. You might be saying, "Lord, I don't feel like myself. I just don't feel right."

You are having spiritual hormone changes. God doesn't *want* you to feel like yourself—*Christ* is being formed in you. Something new and holy is being developed in you, and you won't get through the process without being stretched, expanded, and pressed beyond your normal measure. You're not going to get through this without some stretch marks, but don't stop the process! There is a great reward in the end.

God is looking for individuals and churches who are mature enough to go through a second birth. He is looking for a people who will submit to the stretching, discomfort, and labor required for Christ to be formed in them as a witness to the world. If you say, "Be it unto me," then He will cause you to change as never before. He will speak things into you that sound crazy and absolutely impossible, but don't be alarmed.

He is setting you up for victory on a whole new level, but what He is about to do won't follow any man-pleasing pattern. You won't get there following any preset recipe, formula, or agenda of man. The way of the seed coming from darkness and pressure below to light and glory above is the path of persistent obedience to God and un-yielding faith in His promises. When He speaks, you must be obedient and faithful enough to change without question. For nine months you will stretch, expand, and experience all of the discomforts of change. But then the day will come for your final labor that leads to a miraculous delivery.

8

INHERITANCE OF
THE HEART

The landscape of the American church is littered
with thousands of man-appointed kings and the
shoddy remains of fractured fleshly kingdoms
because we have digressed in our ways all the way back
to the days of Saul, the man who would be king. The
pain we feel is the pain we have brought on ourselves,
but there is a better way.

The church has landed in the same boat with the Israel
that chose Saul, and for the same reasons—both of them
were tired of God's government and His chosen leaders,
especially when those leaders failed to produce godly
sons to carry God's inheritance into the next generation.
The people decided they wanted the more visible (and
more predictable) leadership of their own kings of the flesh.

Now it came to pass when Samuel was old that he
made his sons judges over Israel. The name of his

firstborn was Joel, and the name of his second, Abijah; they were judges in Beersheba. But his sons did not walk in his ways; they turned aside after dishonest gain, took bribes, and perverted justice.

Then all the elders of Israel gathered together and came to Samuel at Ramah, and said to him, "Look, you are old, and your sons do not walk in your ways. Now make us a king to judge us like all the nations."

—1 SAMUEL 8:1–5, ITALICS ADDED

In the latter part of Samuel's life and ministry as a judge over Israel, the nation's elders had a summit meeting and gave Samuel three reasons for their choice of a king over God's appointed judge:

1. "You are old, and it is time for you to move on."

2. "Your sons do not walk in your ways; they do not have your heart. You were a good and right-eous judge, but the sons you expect to inherit the kingdom have turned away to sin. We don't want any part of them."

3. "We want to be like all the other nations and have kings." (It is amazing to see how we too as the body of Christ always want to be like everybody else instead of being what God ordained for us to be.)

YOU CAN HAVE WHAT YOU WANT (AND PAY THE PRICE)

God made it clear that the Israelites were rejecting Him, not Samuel. But Samuel's negligence as a father con-tributed to the problem. God told Samuel to tell Israel, "Okay, you can have a king. You can have what you want." But He must have been thinking, *You would think these people would have learned something with the manna thing in the wilderness.*

Samuel obeyed God's instructions and warned the people in advance about the behavior of the king they would choose, but it didn't do any good. The elders' reply sounds strangely familiar—especially the last part of their answer: "No, but we will have a king over us, that we also may be like all the nations, and that our king may judge us and *go out before us and fight our battles*" (1 Sam. 8:19–20, italics added).

The *people* chose to follow a king, and God gave them Saul. I believe God answered the peoples' request to the letter by choosing Saul according to the criteria of having what "all the other nations had." Saul was tall, dark, and handsome. He was articulate and mighty in looks and deeds.

We shouldn't be amazed when the body of Christ flocks around evangelists and other leaders who look spiritual and regal. Some of these leaders are just as nice on the inside as they are on the outside, but most of the time outward appearance and personal charm have nothing to do with godly character. The problem is that most people don't care, and I'm talking about people in the church as well as nonbelievers. They are too engulfed in the charisma and the exciting events they see unfold under the television lights—the same way Israel was too excited over Saul's selection to consider what it would mean to them for the painful years ahead.

ANYBODY CAN PUT ON A SHOW FOR A LITTLE WHILE

The church is discovering what Israel learned about hastily embracing charismatic leaders who haven't been proven by God's process of maturity. Too often we fail to look at the hearts and lives of our leaders. We need to remember that God rewards us publicly only according to our private lives and deeds. Anybody can put on a show for a little while, but it takes a godly man—whether model material or bald-headed, bow-legged, physically challenged, or downright crazy—to walk in holiness and intimacy by spending private time with God day after day. It didn't take Saul very long to expose the true nature of his heart, and the day came when the prophet of God was sent to confront the foolish king of Israel:

> And Samuel said to Saul, "You have done foolishly. You have not kept the commandment of the LORD your God, which He commanded you. For now the LORD would have established your kingdom over Israel forever. But now your kingdom shall not continue. The LORD has sought for Himself a man after His own heart."
>
> —1 SAMUEL 13:13–14

God wanted to establish His kingdom over Israel forever, but it could only be done one way—God's way. God is looking for men and women who are *after His heart,* and what I am called to say in this chapter is the heart of this book. It may sound revolutionary to some people, but it is God's simple way to build His kingdom—through the inheritance of the heart.

GOD GENERALLY HAS LITTLE TO DO WITH THE PEOPLE'S CHOICE

Saul was forty when he was chosen, and he had everything going for him. Yet from the very beginning he was exposed as a thin-skinned ruler with a hot temper who was given to depression and thoughts of murder. So much for the king the people chose. (I say that the people chose Saul because even though Samuel forewarned them about the king's behavior, they chose to have a king anyway. Saul simply lived out Samuel's prophetic warning.) We live in a nation, and may even attend a local church body that is also being led by men and women—man-centered systems of government—whom the people chose.

In stark contrast, David was born ten years after Saul became king, but he represented God's way—God said he was a man *after His own heart.* I believe we have totally missed or rejected this crucial building block in the body of Christ. God has a sovereign order for the leadership of His flock, and that order is found in the inheritance of the heart. *Only that which is centered and set on the heart of God will last.*

The church has become the murderer of those who have the heart of God. In other words, we have chosen to cling to government and leadership in our churches that constantly try to bring down and remove the men and methods *God has chosen.*

SOME WILL THINK TRUE CHRISTIANITY IS CULTIC

The church has been hindered for countless years and generations because it has openly dismissed this basic foundational building block of God's purpose. Now God is issuing a summons and a challenge to every church body and leader with ears to hear. He is about to bring judgment to the church, and He is doing it for our own good. The things that God wants to do are so opposed to what is going on in the church today that they will cause some church folk to think that we have become cultic. The truth is that God is out to help us become true Christians. What we have now isn't working at all, and we are totally unprepared for what is coming.

> If you have run with the footmen, and they have
>   wearied you,
> Then how can you contend with horses?
> And if in the land of peace,
> In which you trusted, they wearied you,

TAKING OVER

Then how will you do in the floodplain of the Jordan?
—JEREMIAH 12:5

The horses of change are coming, and believers around the world are sensing in their spirits that God has stepped up the tempo, that He is looking for people who can run with Him. We think we have done well surviving our daily trials and temptations in times of peace, but God wants us to realize that the challenges in front of us are bigger than what is behind. The things we have endured and accomplished so far were only strengthening exercises for where we are going.

Due to our mistakes and errors in judgment over the last few centuries, the body of Christ finds itself in a position where we can no longer afford to run to just look good. We are running for the survival and victory of our children and our children's children. God wants every one of us to *inherit His heart*. He also wants us to follow this divine pattern at the local church level where most of us live every day. He wants each of us to inherit the heart and vision of the pastor He has placed over us. (Even though I pastor a church of twenty-two thousand, I also have a pastor because I need a spiritual father's input, counsel, and vision as much as any other believer.)

SOME THINGS ARE NOT UP FOR DEBATE

If you examine God's Word from cover to cover, you will see that for some reason, God always chooses to use men and women to accomplish His will. We like to think that since we have all been made kings and priests in Christ, we don't need leaders anymore. That really isn't up for debate.

The apostle Paul clearly states, "But now God has set the members, each one of them, in the body just as He pleased" (1 Cor. 12:18). The context of this statement makes it clear Paul was answering complaints and concerns about the gifts and leadership rank in the local church. The Bible also commands us to obey those in authority over us, including our church leaders, even though none of them are perfect. (See Romans 13:1-3.)

The Book of Hebrews tells us to "obey those who rule over you, and be submissive, for they watch out for your souls, as those who must give account. Let them do so with joy and not with grief, for that would be unprofitable for you" (13:17). So much for a public forum.

Many people have a serious problem when someone tells them to obey human leaders. They point to all of the leaders who have misused and abused their authority and trust, and I admit that these things happen. David was a man after God's own heart, but there is no way he could be called perfect. David's life history revealed that he was a liar, an adulterer, a cold-blooded murderer, a widely feared professional soldier, and a lousy father. Yet God specifically chose to send us Jesus Christ through David's lineage.

THE TRANSGENERATIONAL TRANSFER OF THE HEART AND SPIRIT OF GOD

You see, God was after a heart, not a perfect attendance record or a no-sin record. Only one Man could ever pull that off. If you inherit the Father's heart, then He will move it from generation to generation in ever-expanding power and glory. It all depends on a transfer of the heart and Spirit of God, and success in the local church setting depends on a transfer of the heart of human leaders to those God places under their care.

Every generation is supposed to be better off than the last generation, but for the first time in history we are looking at a generation that is worse off than the generation that came before. It is all because they did not understand the inheritance of the heart and the transgenerational transfer of vision and knowledge. God wants to move from generation to generation.

God is not interested in just getting you saved, baptized, filled with the Holy Ghost, and moving in power. Yes, you need all of that. However, if you have all of those things *but do not inherit the Father's heart* (or your spiritual father's heart) and pass it on, you will not succeed in God's purpose for your life.

God isn't nearsighted as we are. His vision passes beyond the barrier of time to span *generation after generation.* He sees the beginning from the end. Even before the worlds were made, He could see His Son on the cross. He also saw you entering the world on the day you were born and reading these very words at this moment in time.

It should be no surprise to us that God moves among and upon men *generationally* as well. He is as interested in the well-being of your unborn great-granddaughter as He is in your welfare. The thing He has placed on your heart today will directly affect those who come after you in a later day.

We need to understand that God gives us children as a loan. The Bible tells us children are God's inheritance, and He has given us the responsibility to raise them up to be like arrows shot into the future! (See Psalm 127.) Our sons and daughters must inherit our hearts; they must receive something of the mission and anointing God placed in our hearts. Otherwise these deposits from God will die, and our children will be doomed to start all over *without an inheritance.* (See Proverbs 13:22.)

> Behold, I will send you Elijah the prophet
> Before the coming of the great and dreadful day of
> the LORD.
> And he will turn
> The hearts of the fathers to the children,
> And the hearts of the children to their fathers,
> Lest I come and strike the earth with a curse.
> —MALACHI 4:5–6

We see the transgenerational transfer of power in the Gospels when the "spirit of Elijah" (who died long before) rested on John the Baptist and prompted him to point to Jesus and declare in prophetic power, "Behold! The Lamb of God who takes away the sin of the world!" (John 1:29). John really operated under the spirit and anointing of Elijah as he "prepared the way" for Christ.

Today God is again pouring out the spirit of Elijah, but this time He is pouring it over the body of Christ. He is looking for people who are unafraid to speak with a profound boldness and who will rightly divide the Word of truth.

I'M AFRAID WE GOT WHAT WE ASKED FOR

The very last prophetic words God uttered in the Old Testament through Malachi were, "Lest I come and strike the earth with a curse" (Mal. 4:6). The curse was promised if the hearts didn't turn.

This world is already under a curse. It is evident in our downward spiraling statistics concerning divorce, abortion, incest, rape, violence, corruption, and scandal (even in the church). The greatest indictment of all is that in most cases, you can't tell the Christians apart from the non-Christians—we're all alike. We got what we asked for.

Two people in the Old Testament perfectly depict the nature of this curse, and they were both members of the house of David: Solomon and Absalom.

THE CURSE OF SOLOMON

Later in his life Solomon became a bitter man because, despite all of his wisdom, he failed to prepare for the future:

> Then I hated all my labor in which I had toiled under
> the sun, because I must leave it to the man who will
> come after me. And who knows whether he will be

wise or a fool? Yet he will rule over all my labor in which I toiled and in which I have shown myself wise under the sun. This also is vanity. Therefore I turned my heart and despaired of all the labor in which I had toiled under the sun. For there is a man whose labor is with wisdom, knowledge, and skill; yet he must leave his heritage to a man who has not labored for it. This also is vanity and a great evil.

—ECCLESIASTES 2:18–21

According to God, if you have not prepared someone to take your heart by inheritance, you have raised children (either natural or spiritual) in vain. Solomon was the wisest man who ever lived—even Jesus attested to that. He was the world's first billionaire, yet at the end of his life he said, "Everything is vanity because I have to leave everything that I have to my children who don't have my heart. They will lose what I have acquired."

THE CURSE STOPS RIGHT HERE

We should be preparing a generation for the future, or we will reach the sunset of our lives and find that everything we have done has been in vain. Too many of us are stranded arrows who were forced to start all over. "My grandmama was broke, my mama was broke, and so am I. My grandmama got divorced, my mama got divorced, and so did I." Wait! Somehow, somewhere, somebody in the bloodline has to stand up in Christ and say, "Enough is enough. The curse stops right here, and right here is where God's blessing begins."

Most of us in the body of Christ are losing ground because we don't understand that God goes from faith to faith and from glory to glory (Rom. 1:17; 2 Cor. 3:18). We can sing about it, but we can't walk in it. We can shout about it, but we can't live it. God doesn't want us to start over in every generation. He wants to build family line upon family line, from generation to generation. This goes for your family, and it applies to the family of God as well. Anytime we try to take a shortcut or find an easier way, we cut ourselves off from God's blessing and inherit the curse of Absalom.

THE CURSE OF ABSALOM

Absalom was one of David's greatest sons. He seemed to possess more natural leadership ability than Solomon, and if Absalom hadn't been so crazy, he might have been the one chosen to do what Solomon eventually did. Absalom had so much charisma, confidence, and power that he was able to turn most of the nation against his father, the powerful King David. Now that man was powerful! But instead of inheriting his father's heart, Absalom chose to envy his father's position and power (this sounds like a church soap opera, doesn't it?). Eventually he nearly succeeded in wrenching his father's throne away from him, but in the end he died a rebel's death, suspended between heaven and earth.

> Now Absalom in his lifetime had taken and set up a pillar for himself, which is in the King's Valley. For he said, "I have no son to keep my name in remembrance." He called the pillar after his own name. And to this day it is called Absalom's Monument.
> —2 SAMUEL 18:18

Absalom was childless. His life was barren spiritually, physically, and historically. The only monument he left behind was a shameful legacy of betrayal and rebellion that ended in his untimely death. Absalom cut himself off from his father and failed to train up a son, so he also failed to give anybody the ability to inherit his heart. Absalom was forced to name something after himself, and he put it in a valley where, ironically, it became a lasting monument to his senseless rebellion rather than to his wisdom or charisma.

When we have to start all over because there is no inheritance or generational transfer of the heart, we are forced constantly to put our names on things in the vain hope that somebody will remember us after we are gone. I've settled the question. My success doesn't have anything to do with making a name for myself. I have been given a name to use, and that name is *Jesus*. As for sons, I am a wealthy man. I have a church full of sons and daughters, and I have been blessed with many children in my own house as well.

I have even named my successor to carry on the vision at New Birth Missionary Baptist Church should I leave my assignment early. When I die, my successor will take up the reins and will have the same spirit and the same vision I have, yet he will be expected to take the people to *another level*. That is the secret of the inheritance of the heart. We see it in the way Jesus transferred to us His calling, His anointing, and His Spirit. He expects us to take what He gave us to *another level*. Jesus gave us a perfect picture of the ultimate inheritance of the heart when He said:

> Most assuredly, I say to you, he who believes in Me, the works that I do he will do also; and greater works than these he will do, because I go to My Father. And whatever you ask in My name, that I will do, that the Father may be glorified in the Son.
>
> —JOHN 14:12–13

I am not here just to play around. When I die, the devil will still have to contend with my great-grandchildren, who will be better off than I was in the spirit realm. So if I am giving the devil a little bit of hell today, then by the time he gets to my great-great granddaughter, he is really going to tremble.

THE LOSS OF INHERITANCE IS A CURSE

Absalom's curse is the same curse that is described in Malachi 4:6. When a son fails to turn his heart toward his father, or when a father fails to turn his heart toward his son, a curse descends upon them. This curse is affecting all of us in the body of Christ because it is the failure of a parent to understand and honor the importance of the inheritance of the saints.

The Absalom curse needs to be destroyed, but that poses a problem for "instantaneous saints" because it isn't going to be destroyed in one day or even in one generation. We can begin the process of its destruction today, but since we have allowed the curse to reach floodstage over hundreds of generations, it will take a farsighted people who are willing to go to the flood plain at the Jordan and die one more time. The cure for a generational curse is a godly generational transfer, a transgenerational inheritance of the heart. Our God is a God of generations; that is why He calls Himself the God of Abraham, Isaac, and Jacob.

The most deadly aspect of Absalom's curse is that it limits every generation to a single lifetime of work, and it stops anyone from being able to pick up what those before them learned or accomplished. The only thing it allows to pass through the bloodline are negative aspects of the curse such as physical and spiritual disease, disabilities, and chronic debilitating sins. David's problem with adultery and extreme sexual appetites was passed on to several of his descendants, including Solomon. But Solomon seems to have inherited his father's heart for God's house.

YOUR OWN VISION OR GOD'S VISION?

The Absalom spirit confounds the church with this seemingly spiritual idea that people must find their own vision. On the surface, this statement sounds solid and biblical. We like to rephrase it and tell other people, "We must find the desire for originality and creativity. We must demand our rights. I have a right to get my own vision."

Jesus, on the other hand, took the totally opposite approach:

> Then Jesus answered and said to them, "Most assuredly, I say to you, the Son can do nothing of Himself, but what He sees the Father do; for whatever He does, the Son also does in like manner. For the Father loves the Son, and shows Him all things that He Himself does; and He will show Him greater works than these, that you may marvel. For as the Father raises the dead and gives life to them, even so the Son gives life to whom He will. For the Father judges no one, but has committed all judgment to the Son, that all should honor the Son just as they honor the Father. He who does not honor the Son does not honor the Father who sent Him."
>
> —JOHN 5:19–23

Hear me out, because I am *not* saying, "Don't be creative." I am saying, "Don't be creative first *and then* check with God. Get God's instruction first, and then release your creativity." Most of the time we use creativity as a *substitute* for God.

This also applies to the business world. Most Christian business people try to be creative to sell more. Holy Ghost entrepreneurs, on the other hand, first ask themselves, "Why did God set me up in business? What is God's purpose, and what does the Lord intend for me to do through my business?" Once you know the answers to these questions, you can be truly creative. I guarantee you that whenever you find your divine purpose and operate in what God established, you don't *have* to be as creative because He has already created the market and lined up your customers. He has already provided the way for each of us, but we usurp the way of God because we try to be marketers instead of sons led by the Spirit of God. (See Romans 8:14.)

The same principle applies to our marriages, our family lives, and our ministries. Don't try to save these things; return to the reason or cause that created them in the first place. Once you have an idea why God put you together with your wife and gave the two of you your teenage son, the problems are well on their way to being worked out.

WHAT IS DADDY DOING?

Jesus said, "I cannot do anything that I don't see My Daddy doing." Our children should be saying the same thing and operating the same way. "I don't do a thing that I don't see my Father doing." This is true government, but we don't have it in our homes. That is why our children cannot stand authority. The attitude Jesus had toward His Father and the way He conducted Himself is the prime example of the next generation taking God's purposes to an even higher level.

Jesus took this to what most of us think is an extreme level when He said, "I can of Myself do nothing. As I hear, I judge; and My judgment is righteous, because *I do not seek My own will* but the will of the Father who sent Me" (John 5:30, italics added). Jesus was saying, "I don't have the authority to do anything. I don't seek after My own will. I don't run on My own initiative."

GET THE HEART FROM THE HEAD

I tell the members of my congregation, "You are sons and daughters in the church, and I am father." I don't do this because I'm an egomaniac; I do it because it is biblical. A lot of people don't want to deal with that, but it's in the Bible:

Obey those who rule over you, and be submissive,

for they watch out for your souls, as those who must give account. Let them do so with joy and not with grief, for that would be unprofitable for you.

—Hebrews 13:17

When I first took this stand on biblical order in the church, I heard it all: "It sounds like we're giving somebody too much power." "It sounds cultic." "Sounds like a controlling spirit to me." "Aren't we just giving in to the sovereignty of God a bit much here? Where is our free will?" "I can't go with that. I love to read about Saul, David, and Moses and the three and a half million folk who followed him. Sure, they were obedient some of the time, but I can't do that *because I've got a vision*. I've got something that the Lord told me."

These excuses and complaints highlight one of the most dangerous areas in any church setting. The Absalom spirit delights in repeating its favorite theme—pitting young leadership against old leadership in the church. The younger leadership does not understand that they have to get the *heart* of the spiritual headship to prosper.

Jesus, the Head of the church, the senior Shepherd, plants His vision for a church body in the local under-shepherd of that church. It is this vision, dwelling in the heart of His chosen leader, that is destined to go from generation to generation. But such a vision can *only go on* when it is passed along in godly order from one generation to the next as they all work together to see God's dream come to pass.

If God gave you a vision, then you should know that *whatever God spoke to you, you cannot accomplish in one lifetime*. If you can, it isn't a vision from God. It is a task or a short-term mission. True visions are transgenerational. This may explain why you thought you were crazy. You were trying to figure out how you were going to get all this done before you died, but now you know the vision was never meant to be accomplished in your lifetime alone. You were intended to start it and then pass along the vision of your heart to someone else at God's direction. Name your successor. Give him your heart. Let him understand that he does not have a vision; he is carrying out something from God that you already started.

CHRISTIANS ABORT THEIR VISIONS ABOUT EVERY FORTY YEARS

Even Satan understands the power of generational transfer. Everything the devil learned in one generation he carefully passed on to the next generation of foolish humans. He keeps on acquiring greater darkness and greater numbers of converts, while the Christians keep aborting their visions after forty years, forcing the next generation to enter the war of the Spirit essentially unprepared and unequipped because they have to keep starting all over. In all of the generations since the day of Pentecost in Jerusalem, generation after generation, the church has not changed much at all—unless you measure our incredible lack of power, integrity, miracles, and unity.

The bottom line is this: *God wants you to get His heart so you can pass it on to your children.* When you talk to your children (both spiritual and natural) about your experiences in Christ, don't paint candy-coated pictures of how you came from "there" to "here." The only way you can give God all of the glory is to tell the bad side of the story, too. Don't try to make them think you were a virgin when you know what happened in the back seat of a Volkswagen and what it did to you. Tell them it wasn't worth it! Tell them the truth! Tell them what you have been through so they won't have to suffer the same pain needlessly. Tell them what your grandmama knew, and then explain to them how God has moved and what you have learned in the process.

Then watch them, because they need help. Don't let your living and your mistakes be in vain. Your children—both your natural children and your spiritual children in the body of Christ—are supposed to be better off than you, but that will only come with a deep understanding of how you got "here" from "there."

People—even our children—can relate better to those who are transparent about their failures and shortcomings. We should allow our brokenness and our scars of failure become a visible testimony to God's power and willingness to deliver and transform us. God delights in using broken people to bring wholeness and deliverance to others. He chose David although he was an adulterer and murderer. He chose Moses to confront Pharaoh although he was a murderer with a serious speech impediment. He chose Paul although he was a highly trained Pharisee and one of the most dedicated persecutors of the church. The problem with church folk is that too many of us are looking for another Jesus in the pulpit. I am quick to let my people in on a secret—I am not He.

YOU CAN'T DRIVE THE BUS WITHOUT KEYS

Your church will never be what God called it to be if the believers who are in their forties step aside without having transferred their heart to the next generation. Many great churches and mighty works in cities across this nation are struggling just to survive today. Why? Because when the original founders or fathers of the church passed on, they failed to pass on their vision, heart, and authority to a successor. A good and godly pastor may be struggling to maintain the pastorate, but if the "daddy" God set in place forty years earlier failed to pass along his mantle and heart to this new pastor, he is trying to drive the bus without the keys, without any gas, and without any instructions about the route that bus was assigned to follow!

What I am saying is that God will send ordinary men *into time* endued with extraordinary vision. Their vision will be too great for them to accomplish on their own or even in one lifetime. God wants us to honor His sovereignty and trust His ability to use ordinary flawed men as leaders (those are the only kind available to Him anyway).

Finally, understand that when God sends such leaders into a generation, He doesn't expect those leaders to accomplish His will when they are stuck with hundreds of lone rangers who each think they possess a vision of equal importance to the leader's vision. This takes us back to the "too many cooks spoil the broth" syndrome. Paul made it clear that we don't chose what body part we are to be in the church; it is God who sets us in place as it pleases Him. (See 1 Corinthians 12:14–18.)

The greatest testimony of New Birth Missionary Baptist Church will come after I am dead. This church is supposed to soar and accomplish even greater things tomorrow than what we have accomplished today, and it will be because more than twenty-two thousand grains of wheat fell to the ground and died to their own visions and took up the vision of God as their own. Everything I've learned and experienced says that God delivers His vision for local churches and ministries through the set ministry gift He placed at the head.

A SPIRITUAL FATHER SHOOTS YOU INTO THE FUTURE

Paul spoke forcefully about the existence and importance of spiritual fathers in his first letter to the Corinthians. In fact, Paul's ministry lived on well past his lifetime because of his spiritual sons:

> For though you might have ten thousand instructors in Christ, yet you do not have many fathers; for in Christ Jesus I have begotten you through the gospel. Therefore I urge you, imitate me. For this reason I have sent Timothy to you, who is my beloved and

faithful son in the Lord, who will remind you of my
ways in Christ, as I teach everywhere in every church.
—1 Corinthians 4:15–17

A father is one whom God sovereignly chooses *to pass
on his heart* and spiritual legacy to you as a divine inheritance for the future. A father shoots you into the future
as an arrow of God's anointing, power, and purpose
bearing the accumulated obedience of many generations
in your heart.

I am a firm believer in the priesthood of all believers
and in the finished work of Jesus Christ on the cross. No
man can save us, but it is God's choice that a man should
lead us—and God doesn't ask our opinion about the man
ahead of time. It takes an even greater trust and faith in
God to submit to human leaders when we know they are
flawed just like we are. Yet in the end it all boils down to
one question: Is God really God, or isn't He?

God is saying to us individually, "No more will generation after generation die, but you will go from faith to faith,
from glory to glory." Your grandmama might have been
broke, and you might not have much money, but you are
going to raise up another generation that is going to
unlock the doors to pay it all off! There is a sound rising
of a holy people who are pregnant with purpose. There
is a vision in the house of God that is destined to be
echoed by the multitude of voices of the many-membered
church. Nothing can turn them around. I hear a battle cry
of God.

WILL YOU MISS ME WHEN
I'M GONE?

ive or six years ago I did something every pastor and church leader should do on a regular basis. I asked myself, *If this church building were to burn down, would our community miss us—aside from the easier traffic flow?* I really had to wrestle with that question then because we were spending most of our time talking about world missions and other distant ministries. While mission outreach is very important, I had to admit that our church hadn't really made an impact on our community. We had failed in our first mission.

One of the kingdom principles we would like to forget is that a man must be faithful in what he has been given before he can expect more. (See 1 Corinthians 4:2.) I realized early in my life that God in His sovereignty was directing my steps, and He was orchestrating one divine appointment after another. So, as pastor of New Birth Missionary Baptist Church, God had specifically placed me in that church and that local community to reveal His kingdom. Once that was settled, I knew the mission of the "house." We began to step into line with God's purposes, and we started by putting our own house in order.

This chapter is to the previous chapter what the Book of Acts is to the Gospels. The principles and insights I share here are not based on theoretical what-ifs; they are based on things we have proven in the real world over the last ten years. They are the foundation and driving force of God's favor that catapulted us from a church of three hundred to a growing church of twenty-two thousand in less than a decade (with most of that growth coming in the last three years).

As of this writing, this ministry has boldly carried God's light into inner-city neighborhoods, the criminal court system, public high schools, the Georgia State Senate, the United States Senate, and even into the White House itself. Under God's direction we have challenged antibiblical laws, Supreme Court rulings, state and national legislators, and church leaders with the truth of God's Word. We are under a mandate from God to take the gospel of Jesus into the world without compromise.

Today I can honestly say that metropolitan Atlanta would miss us very much if something caused us to move away or shut down. The New Birth congregation finances and operates vital support programs in the city and pumps large sums of money and thousands of volunteer hours into key areas such as youth offender intervention programs, public school programs, and support and outreach programs for homeless women and children. We are involved in every aspect of life, and we are making a major impact in the Atlanta metropolitan areas.

This, in turn, is causing us to gain major footholds in the city infrastructure. When you are a politician in a major metropolitan area, it isn't wise to dismiss or ignore a highly unified, committed, and motivated group of voters exceeding twenty-two thousand people representing almost every voting precinct in your city. It is even more foolish when a number of the most highly placed political and judicial leaders in the city are deeply committed members and leaders in the church!

From my very first days as a pastor it was clear that the vision God had given me was too large for me to ever accomplish alone. I was in Jonathan's position:

> Then Jonathan said to the young man who bore his armor, "Come, let us go over to the garrison of these uncircumcised; it may be that the LORD will work for us. For nothing restrains the LORD from saving by many or by few."
>
> So his armorbearer said to him, "Do all that is in your heart. Go then; here I am with you, according to your heart...."
>
> And Jonathan climbed up on his hands and knees with his armorbearer after him; and they fell before Jonathan. And as he came after him, his armorbearer killed them. That first slaughter which Jonathan and his armorbearer made was about twenty men within about half an acre of land.
>
> —1 SAMUEL 14:6–7, 13–14

JONATHAN'S ANOINTING PASSED INTO THAT YOUNG MAN

Things were at a standstill until Jonathan received a dose of mountain-moving faith and spoke to the young man who carried his armor. Somehow the anointing upon Jonathan passed into that young man and gave him the courage to do what King Saul and six hundred soldiers would have never done. He agreed unconditionally with Jonathan's impossible vision and marched off with him to take on a whole army!

Jonathan single-handedly knocked twenty people to the ground, but it was his faithful armorbearer who came right behind him and struck the same enemy soldiers with Jonathan's sword and killed them. (Only King Saul and Jonathan had swords or spears at that time according to 1 Samuel 13:22.) The bold strike by Jonathan and his armorbearer seems to have triggered an earthquake of fear (and possibly a genuine earth tremor as God joined in) that put the entire Philistine army on the run. It was only at this point that the disheartened King Saul and the rest of the Israelite army joined in the rout of the enemy. (See 1 Samuel 14:15–20.)

God is looking for an army of faithful armorbearers to follow behind His anointed visionary leaders and strike the winning blow. That translates into a church that is sold out to a vision. The Lord's apostles, prophets, evangelists, pastors, and teachers are anointed to knock down the works of the enemy under the Lord's inspiration. Yet God has ordained that they depend on the Lord's army of faithful armorbearers to come along behind with the weapons these leaders give them and strike these fallen works of evil with a deathblow so they will never rise again.

WE ARE DETERMINED TO TAKE IT TO ANOTHER LEVEL

God has given me, as bishop and senior pastor of New Birth, the vision and the ability to knock the enemy down in certain key areas. But the vision He gave me will never come to pass and impact the Atlanta metropolitan community or the world until the army of armorbearers that God assigned to New Birth rises up with swords in hand. As the people of God rise to the challenge, other leaders and churches will rise up with new courage and vision as well. We have already seen this come to pass to some extent, but we are determined to take it to a new level.

One of the greatest challenges in the body of Christ today is our critical shortage of spiritual "daddies." Where are they? Who is taking the time to raise up sons and daughters and really teach them? Who really understands generational succession? I am convinced that every church leader and local congregation that commit to the task of raising up daddies will be empowered and equipped by God to take over and make a lasting difference in their communities. The church filled with anointed spiritual daddies (and therefore mommies as well) would be sorely missed should they leave an area.

THE MINISTRY GREW AS I DEVELOPED SPIRITUAL SONS

We changed the order of the house at New Birth, and our ministry grew at an incredible pace. But even before that I started developing spiritual sons who naturally did what they saw Daddy do. It was inevitable that our church would make godly waves in our local area, in Atlanta, and later throughout the state of Georgia and the nation. But it all began with sons.

I've already mentioned my conviction that nearly every major problem in society and the church can be traced back to the man. As a natural extension of this conviction and my passion for youth, the Lord directed me to establish a nonprofit youth diversion ministry called Project Impact. It began on a small scale when I obeyed the Lord's leading court system and asked for custody of first-time juvenile offenders who had been convicted of nonviolent crimes. We suggested to the courts that instead of sending these youths to prison, they give them the option of entering Project Impact.

We knew what the courts also know—the prison system does not work as a rehabilitative system. We also understood that only Jesus Christ and God's Word can permanently change and impact these kids' lives for the kingdom. We noticed that a kid can go into the prison system as a shop-lifter and emerge six or twelve months later as a well-trained, big-time bank robber or even a hardened killer.

Our goal was to bring in these young men at risk and tell them that they have destiny. We tell them, "God has you here for a season and a reason. You were born for a purpose, and you were born to be a problem-solver. There is a problem out there that God has created you to solve, and *only you* can solve it. You are that important to God's kingdom."

Up until that time there were a lot of secular and church-based programs that mentored troubled kids in hope of changing their lives. The problem was that as soon as their time was up with these adult mentors, the kids were sent right back into a hellish household. I knew this had to change, so our program was designed not just for the child but for the whole family. When we offer to take a child out of the court system, we require the parents to participate in the program, too. This includes the counseling sessions, classes, and everything else the program involves. Now we are not only talking about saving a child, we are talking about saving the family—and in turn, saving the generations that will follow.

Everyone in a family being considered for Project Impact must sign a covenant stating that they understand why they are there and how many meetings they must attend. If they don't want to commit to the covenant, then they can take their chances with the prison system. If they fail to honor the covenant agreement, they understand that the offender will immediately be returned to the custody of the court or the prison system to serve the original sentence.

We hold a big celebration at the end of the program for everyone who graduates. So far we have an 89 percent success rate, although we are believing God for a 100 percent success rate. Last year we touched over three hundred families with the kingdom of God through this program.

WE DO WHAT WE HAVE TO DO

In this program the most common problem we run into is that the parents can't get to New Birth with their child. So we bought two vans specifically for Project Impact so we could pick up the kids when their parents can't get there. We do what we have to do because it is a priority in the heart of God for our community. Our objective is not to recruit these families as members of New Birth Missionary Baptist Church; it is to teach these families at risk about God's life-changing kingdom principles. Of course, many of these families do join the church along the way, but our chief goal is to make sure they understand how they fit into God's kingdom. We want them to leave us knowing their divine purpose in God, that they were born for a reason, and that they shouldn't waste their time in this life chasing trivial pursuits.

Many of these families are broken or dysfunctional with only a single parent in the home. However, we are so convinced that both brokenness and healing begin with the man of the house that if the man of the house is missing through divorce, separation, or outright abandonment, we try to find him. Many times we are able to convince these missing fathers to participate in the program as well, sometimes right alongside their ex-wives and the child's stepfather.

The program has become national with the headquarters in Ontario, California. I still serve as chairman of the national advisory board of Project Impact, and when New Birth donated five hundred thousand dollars as a challenge grant to the project, it made headlines in the *Atlanta Journal-Constitution* and other newspapers across the country. We are absolutely committed to our youth because they are a major priority with God. This area has dominated our budget almost every year I have been at New Birth, and as a result, we have no shortage of spiritual sons and daughters.

GOD HAS STRONGLY COMMUNICATED HIS DISPLEASURE

Project Impact is only one example of an outreach we

began as a faithful work to the local community that grew to impact the nation. As you have probably noticed, God has strongly communicated to me His displeasure with our nation's growing acceptance of the mythical "separation of church and state" heresy. I am convinced this so-called separation was never the intent of our nation's founding fathers—it is merely a device gradually created by an errant Supreme Court totally apart from historical precedent, tradition, or even the will of the people.

We understand our calling in God to be *leaders* to the nation in matters concerning God's kingdom, and that includes boldly confronting anything—I said *anything*—that raises its head up against the authority of God and His Word. Paul was blunt and to the point when he wrote:

> For the weapons of our warfare are not carnal but mighty in God for pulling down strongholds, casting down arguments and every high thing that exalts itself against the knowledge of God, bringing every thought into captivity to the obedience of Christ.
>
> —2 CORINTHIANS 10:4–5

In 1997 a young student was stabbed during a fight at Southwest DeKalb High School, a local magnet school for gifted students. We were asked by various leaders in the public school system and in the county judicial system to conduct a rally for the heartbroken students. The meeting took place during school hours despite Supreme Court rulings prohibiting public schools from sponsoring religious services. One of our members, Tom Brown, is DeKalb County's top law enforcement officer—DeKalb Public Safety Commissioner. He stood up before the sixteen hundred students (100 percent of the student body) who voluntarily attended the service and said, "Here we are in defiance of the Supreme Court, calling on the name of Jesus Christ."

HUNDREDS OF STUDENTS
CONFESSED CHRIST AS LORD

I preached for twenty-five minutes. I began by telling the students, "God told me to come here because He has chosen Southwest DeKalb [High School] to be His kingdom of high schools." I told them that God had ordained them to be a special group of students and that we had gathered together to sanctify that ordination. Then I said, "I want you to understand that this is the reason we are here; this is the reason the school board allowed us to come; this is the reason the God has ordained this day."

At the end of that seventy-five-minute "motivational assembly," students came forward by the hundreds to confess their faith in Jesus and to receive prayer. As you can imagine, the legal director for the Georgia office of the American Civil Liberties Union (ACLU) was not pleased. We still don't know whether the folks in Washington, D.C., will take us to court or not, but we weighed the cost before we took the stand. We won't back down from the truth of God's Word. There is no "separation of church and state" because God made it all.

TWICE WE CONFRONTED
THE NATION OF ISLAM

We were also compelled by the Lord to lead a number of like-minded churches in taking a stand against two initiatives of the Nation of Islam. That stand put us on the front pages of many of America's newspapers. The first incident happened when Minister Louis Farrakhan issued a nationwide call to all African Americans to attend the so-called Million Man March in Washington. (Nowhere close to that number showed up, but for some reason the number stuck.)

In response, we held a news conference and listed what became known nationally as the Nine Reasons that every

Christian—regardless of color or race—should boycott the event sponsored by the Nation of Islam. Obviously, this didn't make us too popular with the Nation of Islam or even with those segments of the Christian African American population who like to put their loyalty to race and ethnicity ahead of their loyalty to the blood of Christ and the kingdom of God.

Once again we issued the Nine Reasons when Minister Farrakhan called on African Americans to observe a national Day of Atonement (this day is honored by some segments of Islam as well as by observing Jews) by boycotting work, school, and shopping activities. The event was openly billed as a celebration in honor of the second anniversary of the so-called Million Man March. I told the media:

> We cannot support anything that does not have Christ as the center. We have great respect for Minister Farrakhan, but within the confines of the Nation of Islam you will find that it was established as an anti-Christian movement.

Again, this didn't sit well with the sponsors of the event, including some prominent Christian clergymen (some of them from my own denominational family) who failed to recognize the Bible-based differences between the Nation of Islam and the kingdom of God. It doesn't matter—God's Word is true whether it is politically correct or not.

All we are doing is pursuing the vision God gave me as the leader of New Birth Missionary Baptist Church. This pursuit of our destiny can only happen as I impart my heart and vision to others. The mobilization and follow-up on these issues are carried out by my spiritual sons and daughters. Again, this is the key for every local body of Christ who wants to fulfill God's commission to take over instead of being overtaken. We must raise up sons and daughters of the kingdom instead of pouring ourselves into programs, activities, and religious motions outside of God's will.

GOD GAVE ME ANOTHER SON

I have been abundantly blessed with physical sons in my own household, and they are growing powerfully in favor with God and with man. Yet they are still being prepared to fulfill their destiny in the Lord and in the vision. The Lord was preparing spiritual sons as well to step into place in the season I was about to enter.

Shortly after I arrived as the new pastor of New Birth, I was walking down a hallway in our original facility when I observed a young man teaching a teenage Bible study. I was so intrigued by the heart and spirit I sensed in the young man that I made it a point to talk with him after the class. As we talked, I realized this young man had a genuine heart after God combined with a teachable spirit and sincerity of character. It was a very unusual combination for a man of his age.

I encouraged this young man and spent more and more time with him. Finally, I urged him to complete several courses of study and earn several degrees at a local Bible college. When he had completed his work and graduated, I licensed and ordained this young man into the ministry and appointed him to the full-time youth pastorate at New Birth in 1991. The youth ministry has always been very important to me, so I continued to work closely with my young charge. The youth department grew as we drew even closer together in a covenant bond as spiritual father and son.

Over the next five years it became absolutely clear that this young man had caught the vision God had given to me, and he was learning to support me wholeheartedly as I pursued that vision. In 1996 I appointed Jesse Curney III as assistant pastor of New Birth Missionary Baptist

Church, and shortly after that I received a word from the Lord to name Pastor Curney as my successor to the senior pastorate. As the "first son," Pastor Curney continues to enjoy a special relationship with me. It is evident to all that he shares the heart and spirit of his spiritual father, and he helps me carry the load by dealing with the minor issues that arise among his "younger siblings" for me. He is but one of my mighty army of spiritual sons.

GOD GAVE ME AN ELISHA FROM THE IRS

One Sunday morning a number of years ago, a young executive with the Internal Revenue Service was encouraged by some relatives to visit New Birth. He was generally unimpressed with church and religion, but this young man observed the service with tight-lipped patience. He was quietly watching to see if I was going to play the usual money games he had come to expect at offering time. Something he saw that morning made enough of an impression on this young skeptic, however, to bring him back to New Birth for another visit several weeks later. Moved by the Spirit of God and the message delivered that day, the young IRS executive came forward at the altar call to receive Jesus Christ as Lord and Savior and to join the church.

Almost a decade has passed since that day, and Terrance Thornton has become a vital part of the daily operation of the ministry, serving as comptroller of the ministry as well as a source of constant encouragement for me. Along the way, Terrance met and eventually married his lovely wife, Tina, at New Birth. He decided to leave his budding career with the IRS to head up our financial administration. It was under the direction of this gifted son that New Birth was able to fulfill my vision of achieving financial stability and complete legal accountability as a ministry. He also played an important role in several investments that helped New Birth become debt free and acquire the property upon which our new site will be built.

MEET MY SON: A FORMER CONVICT WITH A BOUNTY ON HIS HEAD

Several years ago a drug-addicted gang member and convicted armed robber fled to Atlanta from the south side of Chicago to escape a drug lord's bounty on his head. The only place he could stay was with his uncle, who happened to be the director of the evangelism ministry at New Birth at the time. This young man had run out of options and was nearing the end of his rope.

When I heard about him, I decided to give him a chance as I had so many times before to other young "strays." I offered him a job working with our maintenance man at the time, a wise old saint we simply called Mr. Mack. What happened after that is best told by the young man himself:

> Bishop Long told me to work with Mr. Mack, who was the maintenance man at the time. I walked into the Family Life Center where Mr. Mack was putting together an office desk, and I'll never forget it. He said to me, "There's the toolbox, and there's the instructions. Let me know when you get finished." And then he just left me there! I had never done this kind of thing before, you know? But I said, "Well, I might as well give it a shot."

I am proud to say that Oliver Gilbert, a convicted armed robber, is our operations manager today. Even more important, he is my son in the Lord, and he is a living testimony of God's grace and miracle-working power. Brother Gilbert heads up all the day-to-day logistical operations of our church of twenty-two thousand (which is no small task), and he owns his own carpentry business. He is happily married, and he and his lovely wife, Karen, just moved into their new home with their four children.

Oliver Gilbert is a young man who is a true disciple of the Word of God. He brings a kingdom perspective to life and work. With a prophetic gift and a mighty prayer ministry, Oliver Gilbert raises the standard of excellence, no matter where he is or who is around him.

THIS SON WAS CONVERTED FROM DRUG DEALER TO URBAN MISSIONARY

I have another son in the Spirit who is a former drug dealer and convicted felon; he is also a graduate of the prestigious institutions of Morehouse College and Harvard University. I met this passionate young man one day when he visited the church for the first time, and he immediately joined the church after hearing me preach the first time. (I don't think it was my preaching; it was the voice of the Lord "causing his baby to move.")

The man quickly immersed himself in the ministry of New Birth, teaming up with Pastor Curney, who was serving as our youth pastor at the time. In 1991 this young man, Mark Anthony Mitchell, implemented an innovative outreach group to the inner city that we called Christians In Action. Soon after that, however, rumors and innuendos caused a rift in our father-son relationship, and I decided to let Brother Mark go his way for a time. God had His way, and I eventually endorsed Mark to attend Harvard University to further his theological training in June 1994. Brother Mitchell graduated from Harvard University in June 1997 and came home to New Birth to pick up where he left off. Now an elder in the church, he is giving himself wholeheartedly to what he knows God has called him to do as a true servant of the vision.

Elder Mitchell has a gift for ministering to the disadvantaged, disenfranchised, and discouraged. Inner-city ministry is his forte, and he is the first of my spiritual sons to be a part of a church plant. He now has a clear understanding that his personal call to the urban mission field is the missing piece of expertise and compassion God supplied to fulfill my vision and mission for New Birth Missionary Baptist Church. Only God can take a "perceived menace to society" and miraculously transform him into a catalyst for change in that same society.

THIS MINISTRY IS BUILT UPON SONS AND DAUGHTERS

I've singled out these men and spiritual sons somewhat reluctantly because they represent only a small fraction of the hundreds of spiritual sons and daughters God has given to me and other leaders under my leadership. This ministry is built upon sons and daughters. I confess it. I admit it. I rejoice and glory in Christ over it, and I tell you it is God's way for you and your local church body to take over instead of being overtaken. God begins with one man, a visionary, but His goal is and has always been to see many sons and daughters in His army. Consider this powerful passage in the Book of Hebrews:

> For it was fitting for Him, for whom are all things and by whom are all things, in bringing many sons to glory, to make the captain of their salvation perfect through sufferings. For both He who sanctifies and those who are being sanctified are all of one, for which reason He is not ashamed to call them brethren, saying: "I will declare Your name to My brethren; in the midst of the assembly I will sing praise to You."
>
> And again: "I will put My trust in Him."
>
> And again: "Here am I and the children whom God has given Me."
>
> —HEBREWS 2:10–13

Sometimes I get in a lot of trouble for taking a stand on the biblical pattern of father-son relationships in local church government, and I'm accused of "owning" these young men. This is particularly evident with musicians and artists who are not "covered" or submitted to the leadership God has set in place in a local church. True vision—the kind that changes the world and transforms people from the kingdom of darkness into the kingdom of light—comes from God alone. This kind of vision can only be accomplished *corporately* under the leadership of what I call "set" ministry (meaning the leader whom God *set* or carefully placed in a local church body), and even set ministers need fathers in the faith. (See 1 Corinthians 12:28.)

GOD CALLED US TO BUILD AN ARMY OF SAINTS (NOT A NURSERY)

Everything should be geared around the vision of the house into which God placed you. The Lord gets the word out through sons and daughters, through the army of believers unified around one vision and cause in Christ. The church is weak because her members don't work like that.

We concentrated on raising up New Birth as an army of the Lord rather than as a nursery for the saints. Our entire ministry focus became the development of spiritual sons and daughters in every area, and today we have an army of hard-working soldier-saints clustered around approximately twenty-five spiritual sons who have captured my heart and vision. They all work hand in hand to press forward in the vision of the house. Everything we have today is literally built upon the foundation of godly sons and daughters who were birthed into Christ and raised up in His Word over the years.

The pattern of seeking out sons began when I was in college. I used to drive a school bus in one of the toughest sections of Durham, and I met a young man who was in the third grade then. I had our fraternity sponsor a lot of the kids in the Walltown section, but when this boy heard my voice, *he heard a sound.* I am not his biological father, but I am privileged to tell you I *am* his spiritual dad because something in my voice caused his baby to jump. Everybody he grew up with in his community is either on drugs or dead today. He is the only one in his group to survive, but today he is a preacher because he heard a sound. He now works for me overseeing the maintenance department and several of my recent "additions" (spiritual sons of mine in their late teens and early twenties whom I assigned to work in that department).

Every child needs to hear the voice of a father or a mother speaking what God says about them. Ideally the sound will come from their biological parents, but when it doesn't happen that way, the Spirit of God will sovereignly deposit the desire in the heart of a faithful man or woman to impart His heart to such children. God is just waiting on people like you and me to hear Him speak about a child, to believe it, and then to impart and confirm that thing to the child.

THIS IS THE KEY TO TAKING YOUR CITY

If you want to take your city for God and establish His kingdom, here is the key:

> Like arrows in the hand of a warrior,
> So are the children of one's youth.
> Happy is the man who has his quiver full of them;
> They shall not be ashamed,
> But shall speak with their enemies in the gate.
> —PSALM 127:4–5

If you want to speak fearlessly to the enemies in the gate, be bold enough to gather God's inheritance—your sons and daughters of the kingdom—around you and shoot them as God's arrows into the future. Have the mind of Christ and think long term; don't be limited by the boundaries of your own lifetime or resources. Follow in the footsteps of the Son of God, and build the church of tomorrow on the sons you have today.

10

THE CHURCH IN THE NEW MILLENNIUM

New problems call for new solutions. Old problems that haven't been dealt with by old solutions also demand new solutions. Either way you look at it, the church that enters the new millennium *has to change* or be left behind because God is on the move.

We have done very little to impact our world over the last two thousand years, in spite of the fact that Jesus *finished* His work on Calvary and gave us everything we need to succeed in this life. For the most part, we have coasted along on the coattails of those who went before us, especially the church fathers of the first century who were first and second generation *spiritual sons* of Jesus Christ and the apostles.

It seems that the further we wandered away from the father-to-son and father-to-daughter connection instituted by Jesus, the weaker we became. We chose to embrace the agendas and doctrines of men instead of those that God decreed in His Word. We favored programs over personal discipleship, political intrigue over personal sacrifice and preferring one another. We consistently chose the easy way rather than the right way because when we counted the cost of obedience to God's vision, we thought the cost was too high.

Today our gospel, our faith, and our witness is so watered down that the American church has become a laughingstock to society and the ranks of darkness alike. Enough is enough. It is time for *change*.

GOD IS CHANGING THE SOILED AND FRACTURED CHURCH OF THE PAST

God is bringing judgment to His house before He brings judgment to the world. His perfect will is to see His bride rise up as a glorious church without spot or wrinkle, a shining light demonstrating His glory to all the world. However, this picture of the glorious church is dramatically different from the picture of today's church. So it is clear that God is about to do something to change the soiled and fractured church into something new for a new millennium.

God is out to do more than change our extrabiblical paradigms or ways of thinking; He is out to pull them down and totally destroy them. We've made our own religious ideas and systems into idols that we worship and honor more than God Himself at times. All that is about to come tumbling down. Too often we have tried to build God's house ourselves, or even worse, we've stubbornly chosen to build our church house on a foundation of flesh and place our own name on it. God has a better way, a holier way, and those with ears to hear are hearing a new sound in the earth. It is the sound of God's voice calling, "Come up here" (Rev. 4:1).

So then faith comes by hearing, and hearing by the word of God. But I say, have they not heard? Yes indeed:

"Their sound has gone out to all the earth,
And their words to the ends of the world."
—ROMANS 10:17–18

GOD IS IN NO MOOD TO COMPROMISE OR CODDLE

Whenever a paradigm is challenged, truth and fresh light will "bounce off" the first one or two times. We just don't like to give up our cherished routines, rituals, and rules. This time what we like or don't like just doesn't matter.

God has set His course, and His Word is destined to penetrate and cut through every spiritual barrier that we have built to protect ourselves. The Lord knows that our paradigms and man-made traditions will keep us from moving in the dimension He has ordained. He is out to *take over*, and He is in no mood to compromise or coddle.

God wants to impart this same authority into His sons and daughters, but our religiosity and vain imaginations are blocking the way. For generations we have abandoned His pattern of the inheritance of the heart in our natural families and in the church, and the backwash of our neglect has poisoned the organizations, institutions, and morals of our society and nation even more.

God chose God-fearing men and women to establish this nation. By His sovereignty God established the United States of America; yet because of the failures of the Supreme Court and the executive branch over the last few decades, we have dared to push God away instead of pulling God close. We have rejected truth and refused to inherit the hearts of our forefathers; therefore we have redrafted this nation into something other than what God ordained it to be. The United States today is a mockery before God and a shadow of what we are ordained to be because we have become a nation in rebellion.

The solution to our pain is the same as it has always been: We must get right with God. What was true in Saul's day is still true today. Samuel warned King Saul:

So Samuel said:

"Has the LORD as great delight in burnt offerings and
     sacrifices,
As in obeying the voice of the LORD?
Behold, to obey is better than sacrifice,
And to heed than the fat of rams.
For rebellion is as the sin of witchcraft,
And stubbornness is as iniquity and idolatry.
Because you have rejected the word of the LORD,
He also has rejected you from being king."
                                        —1 SAMUEL 15:22–23

BEWARE A GOVERNMENT GONE WRONG

In Saul's day a government gone wrong nearly destroyed its people. The same thing is happening today. When the house of God, the church, sets itself in order according to God's Word, it will operate in supernatural power, vision, and authority as never before. The true church, the separated church, has every solution the world needs. We have the authority and supernatural wisdom needed to right society's wrongs and bring order wherever there is chaos, but it all begins at the cross.

We are not called to link arms with everybody and every organization that comes along with a good cause. Let them link arms with us *after* they lay aside their private agendas and alliances with devils, for we have something far superior to any good cause or noble end. We are the people of God; we carry the Spirit of the Savior and the power of the Creator. We serve the Lamb of God who takes away the sins of the world. We come in the name of the King of kings and the Lord of lords, not merely in the name of a good cause or some nice idea.

I've gone into great detail about the importance of raising up sons and daughters in the kingdom and how this principle has become the foundation of my life and ministry. God intends to carry this pattern to the highest levels of the church and to every area of our society. His preordained plan and method is to *take over*. I know this makes our critics nervous, and I want to say that *they should be nervous.* Their only consolation is that we intend to take over through love, not violence or coercion.

In my own experience I've noticed that God has taken my ministry to "sons" to a new level. Recently I was asked to speak at a conference where I found myself thinking, *Lord, did I miss You in this? Should I be at home?* I didn't even know what the Lord wanted me to say. In fact, I switched messages just before I stood to minister.

Evidently I landed on the message God wanted me to preach because that church has been in revival ever since that service. They told me later that the word that really spoke to them came through me. God set people free of lust and drugs, and He put marriages back together that night. Everybody was at the altar on their faces before God.

"THAT'S MY DADDY"

I realized God was up to something in my "fathering" ministry from the moment I arrived at that church. I had never met the pastor before, but when I walked into the church, shook this man's hand, and gave him a hug, we were immediately joined together in the Spirit. After I ministered in that powerful service, I was ready to go to the hotel and go to bed. I put on a jogging suit and sneakers for the ride back to the hotel, but God led me right back in front of that church. Even though it was midnight, the pastor had asked the congregation to wait for me.

This pastor stood up in front of his congregation and said, "The Lord spoke to me tonight, and I have heard something. I have never met this man before," he said as he turned toward me, *"but that's my daddy."* In that moment this church of more than five thousand began to leap for joy because they too heard the *sound* that was coming from my voice. That night the entire congregation and its pastor submitted to my spiritual headship—but not because I asked them to do so. Why did they do it? *It was because they heard a sound.*

There was no interview. There was no questioning. There was no debate or discussion. This pastor did not have to do it, but he heard a sound. I'm seeing this same process take place everywhere God sends me. Very often, just as soon as I finish ministering God's Word, a pastor will say, "Will you be my daddy? I realize I have to submit somewhere because I have to be covered. I hear that same thing you are hearing, but I need to be led." I don't know if you realize it, but this kind of thing can only happen because God is behind it. (I can guarantee that I don't engineer these events.)

LEAVE COMPROMISE AND PAST FAILURE BEHIND

I am convinced that millions of Christians around the world are hearing God say the same things I have heard. I also know that I was preordained to write this book to confirm these things and to equip the body of Christ for the new millennium. I am not the only leader commanded to speak, but I am the only one I can personally answer for.

I urge you by the Spirit of God to lay aside every weight that has so easily entangled you in the past. Make a clean break from the past today. Press forward for the mark of your high calling in Christ Jesus. It is time to rise and answer God's call to a higher standard. It is time to leave compromise and concerns about past failures behind. It is time to take over.

I want to share ten principles for life and ministry that God has given me from His Word. I have practiced these principles by His grace, and they are proven in battle. My sons and daughters in the Lord have also practiced these principles and have proven them in their own lives and ministry. If you follow these principles drawn from God's

Word, you will be moved into position for war, well equipped for leadership in your community.

TEN KEY BIBLE PRINCIPLES FOR LIFE AND MINISTRY

1. Tune out others' opinions.

When we get delivered from worrying about what people are thinking or saying about us, we will be free to be whom God has made us and called us to be. We won't be locked into trying to please people. When we try to please people, two things happen to us: We drive ourselves crazy trying to please everybody, and we never truly please God because we are not be operating in our God-ordained assignment.

2. Be transparent.

Your message comes from the "mess" from which God has delivered you. If you can be secure enough to minister out of your own brokenness, mistakes, and challenges, then you will free up someone else in your congregation. That person will see your life and deliverance from failure as *living proof* that God is able and willing to free *him or her* from the same situation you were in. (See 2 Corinthians 1:3–6; 4:15; 12:9.)

3. Avoid tradition.

Too many times we get so locked into our printed programs or our usual order of worship that we run the risk of missing out on what the Spirit of God wants us to say or do. Our man-made traditions often don't have anything to do with the Spirit or the presence of God. Be flexible enough to follow what God wants to do. (See Isaiah 43:19; 48:6; Matthew 15:3; Mark 7:13; Colossians 2:8; 1 Peter 1:18.)

4. Try something new or something you have never done before.

I am not afraid of trying something and failing. I am,

however, afraid of succeeding at the wrong thing. I don't want to stand before God to explain why I misused the talents and time He gave me by focusing on the wrong thing.

5. Remain thirsty.

Keep seeking after God. Pursue His presence; hunger to do His will. Never be satisfied. Always strive for excellence. Never become comfortable where you are. Read the Bible for your own personal growth, not just for sermons. Always seek to grow. Be so thirsty that you make others around you thirsty as well!

6. Trust in God's sovereignty.

I no longer have to worry about coming up with cute titles or new sermon ideas. All I have to do is find God. When I find Him, I have absolute confidence that He will reveal to me what He has already predetermined before the foundations of the world. When I lean totally on Him, He always comes through.

7. Tell the truth.

Do not compromise or water down the gospel. God never called the church to coexist. The enemy has come into our society like a flood, and the world is looking for a standard to be raised. God has not changed His mind since He gave man dominion in Genesis 1:26. As a matter of fact, the Great Commission is only an extension of the dominion the church is supposed to exercise. When we give people God's truth, it may hurt, but they will come back for more because of the lack of truth in our society.

8. Understand the reality and importance of the transference of spirit.

This is an important concept in the Bible that you cannot afford to ignore or dismiss. Just as Elisha got a double portion of Elijah's (not God's) spirit, we need to pass ours on as well.

- First, *find your spiritual father,* a mentor, through prayer. He should be someone older and wiser who teaches you how to grow into your potential in Christ by speaking life into you. He should be someone who makes your "baby jump" (just as the presence of Christ in Mary's womb made Elizabeth's baby, the future John the Baptist, jump). Capture his spirit, use his wisdom, and submit to his God-given vision.

- Second, *transfer what God has given you to someone else.* Remember, if your vision can be completed in your lifetime, God didn't give it to you. Share what you know and have learned with others. (See 2 Timothy 2:2.)

9. *Temper your ministry with love.*

Your love for people should be evident. Love them, hug them, and openly show them you care. Showing Jesus' love for others should be our motivation. Remember, He loved prostitutes and sinners, and He didn't mind showing it in front of everyone.

10. *Stay thankful.*

We run a serious risk of becoming ungrateful like the children of Israel when we let the routine of life wear down the luster of God's precious gifts of life, family, ministry, gifting, and so on. (See 1 Corinthians 10:1–5, 10.) God sees our complaining and ungratefulness in the same light as He sees sexual immorality! Always remember to be grateful to God for what He has done for you. We need to echo the heart and prayer of the apostle Paul who said, "And I thank Christ Jesus our Lord who has enabled me, because He counted me faithful, putting me into the ministry" (1 Tim. 1:12).

I SEE A CHURCH READY TO RUN
TO THE BATTLE!

Let me describe the church of the new millennium that I see in my spirit. I see a body of Christians who are fit and ready to run to the battle, whether it is convenient or not. These believers volunteered for the fight, even though they fully understand that the kingdom of God suffers violence, and the violent take it by force. They refuse to be distracted or ruffled by minor nuisances such as traffic problems and opposition from the hesitant saints at First Church around the corner. They are too focused on rebuking the enemy and redeeming the souls of children, prostitutes, and the drug lords who foolishly decided to set up a crack house in God's territory. They sense the time for battle is near, and they are eager to run at the Master's command.

These members of the remnant church heard the rumors long ago; they heard the sounds of God raising up an army, and they were quick to heed His call. No matter where you go, you can find them by the millions saying, "I hear that sound."

I see the princes and kings of this world in the twenty-first century looking to the glorious church because of her glory and power. This church in the new millennium is the head and not the tail. I see the musicians of the world once again copying the music of the church because they are searching for "the sound" that makes the people one. The members of this glorious church will again have a well-earned reputation as "the original creators" because they have learned to tap into the unlimited creativity of the original Creator, their Father.

This is the picture I see of the church that God wants to take into the next century. This is the church of the new millennium He has ordained to *take over* as "the head and not the tail," as "above and not beneath." (See Deuteronomy 28:13.) I envision kingdom-controlled businesses, banks, governmental bodies, schools, families, and churches.

Sadly, at this point most of us are too overtaken and over-run to make a claim on Satan's territory. I am convinced that the American church in particular will have to go through just a little more pain, but there is a great incentive for us to press through this time of cleansing and preparation. God has made us pregnant with His purpose, and though we are still laboring to deliver God's covering glory to the earth, that day of deliverance is coming! On that day, God's glorious church will be over-joyed, and all of our painful labor will be forgotten when we are overflowing in His glory.

WE FEEL THE PANGS OF LABOR SEIZING OUR SOULS

Before that great day God has ordained the births of mil-lions of sons and daughters of the Spirit into the earth. You see, God has made us pregnant individually as well as cor-porately. We feel the pangs of labor seizing our souls—God is telling us it is time to be stretched and enlarged.

We must be willing to change, to discard the old to make room for the new. We must lay aside our ways to receive His ways in our hearts. We must expand our houses to take in sons and daughters we never knew existed, and then we must impart our hearts and inheritance to them. As we say to the Lord individually and corporately, "Be it unto me according to Thy Word," a new day and a new millennium will dawn. A mighty army will be born, and we will all share the same heart and vision in Jesus Christ to *take over*.

> *I am here to take over, not to take sides.*
> *I have come to take over, and I have no*
> *room for compromise.*
> *This is a whole new way of life; this is a*
> *whole new way of thinking.*
> *This is a whole new way of operation,*
> *and when you get that settled,*
> *You're presenting kingdom.*

Bishop Eddie Long Ministries

P. O. Box 2607
Atlanta, GA 30301
1-800-985-3787
1-770-482-1125 (FAX)
Website address: http://www.newbirth.org
E-mail: kingdom@newbirth.org

BOOKS		PRICE
I DON'T WANT DELILAH…I NEED YOU		$11
AUDIO TAPE SERIES		**PRICE**
In Between	NEW!!	$15
SEE	NEW!!	$10
Life's Survival Kit	NEW!!	$30
From a Family to a Nation	NEW!!	$10
This Gospel	NEW!!	$15
Your Vision Is Too Small		$10
Inheritance of the Heart		$10
Generational Wealth		$15
Let's Talk About Sex		$15
VIDEO TAPE SERIES		**PRICE**
SEE	NEW!!	$30
From a Family to a Nation	NEW!!	$30
This Gospel	NEW!!	$20
Your Vision Is Too Small		$20
Generational Wealth		$20
Let's Talk About Sex		$20
SINGLE AUDIO/SINGLE VIDEO		**PRICE**
I DON'T WANT DELILAH…I NEED YOU!		$6
I DON'T WANT DELILAH…I NEED YOU! CD		$10
Destroying the Image		$6
Back to the Future		$6
God's Open Door		$6
The Signs of the Times	NEW!!	$6